IN SEARCH OF THE BUFFALO

The Story of J. Wright Mooar

by Charles G. Anderson

Artwork by Marcus K. Anderson

Pioneer Press
Union City, Tennessee
1996

All Rights Reserved. No part of this publication may be reproduced, stored in a retrieval system or transmitted in any form or by any means, electrical, mechanical or otherwise without first seeking the written permission of the publisher.

First Edition - Copyright © 1974 by Pioneer Book Publishers, Inc., Seagraves, Texas.

Second, Revised Edition - Copyright © 1996
     by Charles G. Anderson.
Pioneer Press, P.O. Box 684, Union City, TN 38281

Anderson, Charles G.
   In search of the buffalo: the story of J. Wright Mooar
   by Charles G. Anderson.
        p.   cm. -- (Buffalo Hunters)
   Includes endnotes, bibliography and index.

   ISBN 1-877704-24-5 (sc: coated paper)
   1. Mooar, J. Wright, 1851-1940, 2. Buffalo hunter.
      3. Texas History.   4, Kansas History   5. Biography.

Original artwork by Marcus Kendall Anderson, Snyder, Texas, ca. 1974.

FRONT COVER: John Wesley Mooar (left) and J. Wright Mooar (right) ca. 1910, display the hide of the white buffalo which Wright killed in Scurry County, Texas October 7, 1876. (Photo courtesy Scurry County Museum, Snyder, Texas)

PREFACE

"If you don't know where you have been, how can you decide where you are going?"
Hugh Boren, Jr., Chairman
Scurry County Historical
Survey Committee - 1974

    This comment was made in the preface for the first edition of this biography of J. Wright Mooar, one of the best known Texas buffalo hunters of the last half of the 19th century.
    Buffalo hunters were courageous entrepreneurs, operating vagabond style small businesses in a time and place where each day one lived was a miracle. Some, like Mooar, became fairly wealthy from their dangerous endeavors, retired from their harrowing days on the plains, and lived in comfort to ripe old ages.
    This book is the primary study of the life of J. Wright Mooar, his family and associates. Mooar was one of the few hunters fortunate enough to kill a white buffalo, thus ensuring his place in Texas - and buffalo hunting - history.
    After living in Colorado (City), Texas for a few years, Mooar settled in Snyder near the spot where he saw the white buffalo. He and his brother, John Wesley, became well-to-do ranchers and businessmen both in Colorado (City) and in Snyder. John lived out his days at Colorado (City), and both men were recognized as leaders in their communities.
    The Scurry County Texas Historical Survey Committee fully endorsed this book when it first appeared in 1974, and has continued to promote the work, testimony to its accuracy and to the thoroughness with which Mr. Anderson has conducted his research.

*A Good Man Leaveth An Inheritance
To His Children's Children.
Proverbs 13:22*

Dedicated To

B. K. Newhouse

He carved a place for himself and his family along the banks of the Clear Fork of the Brazos. The buffalo and Indians were gone when he arrived in West Texas, but there were other challenges here and he faced them as a true pioneer.

ACKNOWLEDGEMENTS

Many of J. Wright Mooar's stories have been recorded in newspapers and magazines at various times. They were always reported exactly as Mr. Mooar remembered them, and he never grew tired of relating each and every incident. Young boys, who are now old men, still tell of sitting at Mooar's feet as he spun his tales of adventure. The young lads gathered in the late evening to hear how Indians and buffalo hunters fought for possession of the great Texas herd. These same stories can be found today in newspapers, magazines and in Mooar's personal notes.

I have tried to retrace each one of Mooar's stories with additional research, and I have added details to events where new evidence has been found. Dates and times have been thoroughly researched, and each story has been kept as historically accurate as possible. I have collected numerous photographs to show the important people and places that helped to make J. Wright Mooar's adventures more memorable events.

My sincere thanks are extended to many people who had a hand in producing this book. I owe a special debt of gratitude to Judy Hays, granddaughter of J. Wright Mooar, for her permission to publish his stories in book form, and for the use of other photos and materials. Mrs. Hays was also a great help in finalizing the first book for publication, adding much new information on her grandfather and his buffalo hunting exploits.

Mr. Hugh Boren, Jr., chairman of the Scurry County Historical Survey Committee, advised me on numerous occasions. He opened his own research files to me, much of the data having been recorded by Mr. Mooar shortly before his death, and collected by Boren at that time.

June McGlaun, Snyder teacher and member of the Scurry County Historical Survey Committee, helped revise materials and prepare it for publication. Georgene Galloway and Phil Kelly have been most helpful in locating sources during my research.

Roy Hendrix worked on the Mooar Ranch during the 1920s, and related to me many stories of Mooar, filling in details that had not been previously recorded.

Nelda Bills and Ernest Sears of the Scurry County Museum Association, helped locate photographs and other materials necessary to the book. I appreciate their time, effort and advice. My special thanks to Mrs. Bruce Campbell and the Colorado City Museum Association for their help in finding materials from that town.

I appreciated the endorsement of the Scurry County Historical Survey Committee when I began this project in 1970, and its support has been a source of continued encouragement.

My special appreciation is extended to the Scurry County Library staff for their help during my research into the life of J. Wright Mooar.

I called on numerous Scurry Countians during my research checking dates, places and events. Among those were Frank Pruitt, Red Walker, Esther Boren, Jean Everett, Lida Rhoades, Wanda Falls, Elaine Rosser Lambert, and Jack Craft. Their assistance in readying this book for publication is much appreciated.

Numerous historical societies and museums have been instrumental in supplying photographs that illustrate Mooar's life. They are: Archives for the American Southwest, Texas Tech Univ., Lubbock, TX; National Archives, Washington, DC; Boot Hill Museum, Dodge City, KS; Library of Congress, Washington, DC; Colorado City Museum, Colorado City, TX; The National Forest Service, Washington, DC; Amon Carter Museum, Ft.Worth, TX; Cy Martin and the Hart Publishing Co., New York, NY; Old Jail Art Center & Archives, Albany, TX; American Museum of Natural History, Washington, DC; Kansas State Historical Society, Topeka, KS; Smithsonian Institution, Washington, DC; the Abilene Reporter News, Abilene, TX; Univ. of Oklahoma, Norman, OK; Snyder Daily News, Snyder, TX.

And, my special thanks to my editor, Sharon Cunningham of Pioneer Press, Union City, Tennessee, for challenging and guiding me in the revision of this book. I am indebted to Sharon for her many hours devoted to shepherding this second edition of the biography of J. Wright Mooar to its final publication.

INTRODUCTION

During the period of 1870-1880, many changes and major conflicts were visited upon the American West. J. Wright Mooar spent those ten years living in dugouts on the plains of Texas, Indian Territory and Kansas during Indian uprisings and through the great slaughter of the buffalo by white hunters.

In those ten years, almost four million American Bison were killed by hunters; Mooar said he contributed 22,000 of that number himself. He is best known, though, for his killing of an albino buffalo on Deep Creek near Snyder, Texas on October 7, 1876.

J. Wright Mooar said he saw millions of buffalo on the banks of the Arkansas River on August 10, 1872; many people have questioned his claim, but after careful examination of historical documents, I personally believe that Mooar was correct in his estimation of the great herd. Other historians, as well, speak of the millions of bison on the Great Plains during the 1870s.

The purpose for writing this book is to present the exploits of Mooar in simple story form. For in reading about this man, one has to feel a greater pride in the civilization of the American West. He never regretted the killing of the buffalo, because he knew it was necessary to bring civilization to the Western Plains. While Mooar fought Indians on many occasions, Quanah Parker, Whirlwind and other Plains Indians later became his friends. Mooar never apologized fo rhis part in the buffalo extermination, and he never tried to explain it to either his white or red friends.

Not only was Mooar seeking adventure, buffalo hides and the sales of meat became a fruitful business enterprise. But, hunting buffalo was something that he enjoyed and wanted to do; it was all the adventure and excitement he had dreamed of - and he lived every minute to the fullest.

These are the adventures of J. Wright Mooar, a boy from Vermont, who quickly became a man when he landed his first job as a wood chopper with the army at Ft. Hays, Kansas in 1870.

The dates, places and names of people are as accurate as they have been recorded in various contemporary documents; newspapers, magazines, books, family Bibles, and Mooar's own personal notes.

J. Wright Mooar was a hunter who longed for adventure in the West and found it following the great buffalo herds. When they were decimated by overhunting, Mooar was lonesome for them and missed the wild old days of high adventure, but his love for living on the Western Plains never faded.

My hope is that as you read J. Wright Mooar's biography, you will experience the same sense of excitement he felt when he went *In Search of the Buffalo*.

                                          Charles G. Anderson
                                          Snyder, Texas
                                          1996

"Wonder how much farther that kid is going, to try to find where the sun goes down?"

Spoken of J. Wright Mooar by a fellow hunter.
Quoted by Mooar in *Holland's*, May, 1933, p. 11

Josiah Wright Mooar c.1890
(Photo courtesy Judy Hays)

CONTENTS

Preface iii
Dedication iv
Acknowledgements v
Introduction vii

I.	Boyhood Days 13
II.	Mooar Becomes a Hunter 18
III.	Two Lawless Companions 26
IV.	Escape From Death 29
V.	Wright Sees The Great Herd 31
VI.	Lost In A Blizzard 34
VII.	A Decision To Move - Let's Get Out Of Dodge 36
VIII.	The Panhandle Expedition 43
IX.	Unrest At Adobe Walls 48
X.	Fast Trip To Red Deer Creek 51
XI.	The Battle Of Adobe Walls 54
XII.	Back To Dodge City 66
XIII.	Chief Whirlwind 68
XIV.	Farewell To The Chief 73
XV.	Texas, Vermont, Texas 76
XVI.	The White Buffalo 82
XVII.	Winter In Deep Creek Country 89
XVIII.	Other Ventures 95
XIX.	Wright Finds The Last Great Buffalo Herd 99
XX.	Westward To Arizona 101

Epilogue 104
Appendix I - J. Wright Mooar's Guns 115
Appendix II - A West Texas Photo Album 120
White Buffalo Poem 132
End Notes 134
Bibliography 135
Index 138

Chapter 1

Boyhood Days
1851-1870

When J. Wright Mooar became a buffalo hunter in the great American West, a fellow hunter once said of him, "Wonder how much farther that kid is going, to try to find where the sun goes down?" Mooar did just that; he found 'where the sun went down' on the great plains of Texas, and made his home there.

The new land, with Deep Creek cutting through the tall prairie grass and the Caprock looming in the west, would have been strange and different to Mooar's Scottish ancestors. After first coming to New York, the Mooar clan moved to the wilds of Vermont. There, they found the same peaceful atmosphere in the green hills that they remembered from their native Scotland.

The Mooars went about the business of farming like most people in their community at that time. Hardwood, too, was a growing business in Vermont during this period, and Wright's father worked in a hardwood factory to supplement the family income.

The small agricultural village of Pownal soon grew into a town, but by the middle 1800s, the village experienced the same restlessness which swept the entire country on the eve of the Civil War when many people looked toward the uninhabited West.

Josiah Wright Mooar, called Wright by his family, was born August 10, 1851 at the family farm house of John Allen and Esther K. Mooar. The peaceful setting of Mooar's birth was a direct contrast to the places of his future adventures in the American West. Everyone was talking about the West during this period, but no one suspected that J. Wright Mooar would become a major player in its flamboyant history.

Wright often reflected on his experiences in Pownal and compared them with his adventures among the great buffalo herds and the Indians on the Western Plains. His days of relative ease and security in Vermont had not conditioned him for those adventures, but he quickly learned to handle each situation that came to him.

J. WRIGHT MOOAR was born in this Pownal, Vermont farmhouse August 10, 1851. (Photo courtesy Archives for the American Southwest, Texas Tech University, Lubbock, Texas)

The Civil War ended when Wright was fourteen years old. He listened to soldiers as they returned to their homes and told of their travels. New ways of life had been forced upon many of them, and they, too, had become restless spirits. The stories of General Randolph B. Marcy's expedition into the West had reached Pownal, and Wright read every account available. In 1856, future Civil War General Robert E. Lee, a Lieutenant Colonel in the Federal army, was assigned to Camp Cooper on the West Texas plains, and had explored the same area, searching for a spot to locate a new fort. Lee, too, had written glowing reports of the American West.

GEN. RANDOLPH MARCY explored the Deep Creek area of west Texas in 1849. His explorations paved the way for Mooar and others who came to Texas to hunt buffalo. (Photo courtesy Scurry County Museum, Snyder, Texas)

Returning veterans found it difficult after being in combat to adjust to the slow, pastoral life in Pownal, and headed West. Mooar, too, grew more restless as he reached his late teens, and by the summer of 1868, when he was seventeen, J. Wright Mooar left home and seek his own adventures. Traveling to Chicago, he found work as a street car conductor, but this was not the adventure he longed for and the young man remained unsettled.

Chicago newspapers carried stories of the unconquered West and Mooar read every account. Disappointed, homesick and bored, he returned to Vermont where he worked in a weaving mill during that winter.

MOOAR WAS JUST 19 in the fall of 1870 when he began chopping wood for the army at Fort Hays, Kansas. This 1873 photograph, taken about the time Mooar was working in Kansas, shows the barracks, mess hall, kitchen and wash houses at the fort. (Photo courtesy U.S. War Dept., General Staff, National Archives, Washignton, D.C.)

    Still not satisfied and growing even more restless, Wright left Vermont again, this time stopping in Rochelle, Illinois. The town was experiencing a spurt of growth and new houses were needed. During the spring of 1870, Mooar worked as a carpenter in Rochelle. He tried to convey excitement in letters to his parents, but this work proved as dull and unchallenging to Mooar as that in Chicago had been.

    In the summer of 1870, he quit his job and headed for Fort Hays, Kansas. Mooar was just nineteen years old when he applied for a job as a wood chopper with the army at the fort. Here, he realized, was a part of the great West he had been reading about for five years. Mooar listened to accounts of buffalo hunting brought to the fort by soldiers. He saw maps of expeditions into the buffalo country, and longed to go there himself. "The herds darken the prairie," they would say. "Millions are passing through the great Western Plains."

Mooar could scarcely credit these stories, but yearned for something more than wood chopping, so the accounts were worth investigating. Soon his work at the fort was as uninteresting as his previous jobs had been, and he was again the restless young man with adventure in his heart.

Unable to resist any longer, in late 1870, Wright Mooar quit his wood cutting job and began hunting buffalo on the plains near Fort Hays. His Great Western Adventure had begun...

MAP SHOWS J. WRIGHT MOOAR'S route of travel in 1868-1870, from his home in Pownal, Vermont to Ft. Hays, Kansas, where he began his Great Western Adventure.

Chapter 2

Mooar Becomes a Hunter
1870-1872

Buffalo was the main source of meat for settlers in Kansas, and Mooar found pleasure and adventure in hunting them. Mostly, though, it was profitable. Many new settlers moved into the Fort Hays area during the winter of 1870, and they needed meat for survival. Mooar was glad to sell it to them.

There was a terrible waste of buffalo meat on the Kansas Plains. Hunters killed the animals, took a hind quarter and left the rest of the meat and the hide to rot. Mooar could not understand the reason for such destruction.

The Plains Indians never wasted this primary source of food and shelter. The buffalo skins were used for tipi covers, robes, moccasins, mittens, caps and whatever else could be made from the furry hides. Buffalo was the Indians' meat staple. The horns were made into eating and cooking utensils, hoofs were boiled down for glue, and the tail became a fly swat or was used for ornamentation of the Indian garments. A prairie staple called "boudins," was made by stuffing the buff's intestine with seasoned meat, which was then roasted or boiled. Nothing from the buffalo was wasted by the nomadic Plains Indians, who followed the big herds on their annual migrations.

The white buffalo hunter at this time had found little use for the skins. A few had sent hides to English firms, but American companies were not interested, and most of the hunters were primarily interested in selling the meat to settlers. Mooar began saving hides in hopes of locating a market among the English firms, but on impulse, he sent a few to this brother in New York. He hoped that John Wesley might find a market there.

John Mooar also had a great interest in the West. He and Wright corresponded regularly and his desire to go west was rekindled on receipt of each letter. John had found security in New York in the jewelry business. He arrived in New York at the age of fifteen and got a job as an errand boy for Randall H. Green & Sons, brokers at 98 Wall Street. Later, he was employed by J.J. and J.M.

Richards, large manufacturers of jewelry. He studied diligently in his spare time and graduated with a degree of Master of Accounts from Eastman's Business College in Poughkeepsie, New York. Eastman's was considered the best college of its type in the country at that time. When Wright's glowing accounts of the West reached John, he felt his business on Wall Street to be of less importance.

IN THE EARLY 1870S, the great buffalo slaughter had begun. Animals were killed, only the hind quarters taken and the rest of the meat and hide left to spoil. This photograph, taken in the 1870s, shows the extent of this waste. ((Photo courtesy Boot Hill Museum, Dodge City, Kansas)

Fifty-seven raw buffalo hides arrived in New York and John hauled them down Broadway to Pine Street. The sight created such a commotion that they were sold almost immediately. Two tanners from Pennvylvania offered $3.50 each for the hides, fourteen cents a pound. John accepted the first offer and immediately sent a letter to Wright telling him of their success.

The Pennsylvania tanners were elated with their experiments with the skins. They learned that buffalo hides could be easily tanned and made into useful leather products, and soon also found a ready market in lap robes. Easterners liked the robe's heavy warmth, and

JOHN WESLEY MOOAR, June 12, 1846-May 24, 1918. Educated in the East, John soon joined Wright to begin a new experience among the buffalo hunters on the Kansas Plains. He was a buffalo hunter, too, but never achieved the fame of his older brother. (Photo courtesy Lydia Louise Mooar, Marietta, Georgia, John Wesley's daughter. This photo was sent the author by Miss Mooar in May, 1974. She died shortly thereafter; her letters and memorabilia are housed at the Texas Tech Historical Museum, Lubbock, Texas).

HUNTING ON THE PLAINS. This 1871 Currier & Ives print published in New York, shows hunters as they killed the great beasts of the Plains. John Wesley Mooar was in New York at this time; pictures and accounts such as this one, along with letters from his brother, Wright, persuaded him to give up a lucrative position on Wall Street and join Wright in Dodge City. (Photo courtesy Library of Congress, Washington, D.C.)

it was a novelty from the West.

The tanners ordered two thousand hides to be delivered as soon as possible. John sent word to Wright, resigned his position on Wall Street and left New York for Dodge City, Kansas. There, in the fall of 1872, Wright, John, and a cousin, Charles Wright, formed a buffalo hunting company. Wright loaned John and Charles each $250 to establish the company. The men agreed together to name the company Mooar Brothers and Wright; each man would share equally in the profits. Under the arrangement, Wright would hunt and help skin the buffalo, and John and Charles would be the freighters, do the marketing and look after the camp.

The new enterprise did not waste time in securing its share of the new industry in buffalo by-products. Settlers and railroad company employees readily bought the meat, and Eastern markets wanted the hides for industrial use.

The Mooars established their company headquarters in Dodge City, but hunting camps were set up throughout Kansas and would eventually move their undertaking into Texas. Harvesting the great beasts of the Western Plains was hitting its stride and J. Wright Mooar and his company were a vital part of the event.

THE MOOARS ESTABLISHED their company headquarters at Dodge City, Kansas. This picture shows the business section of the old fort. The right end of the long stone building housed a saloon and the left, a billiard hall. The next building was the store of R.M. Wright & A.J. Anthony. The photo was made in 1872, the year the Mooars set up headquarters there. (Photo courtesy Boot Hill Museum, Dodge City, Kansas)

AN 1871 WOOD ENGRAVING shows hunters shooting buffalo on the line of the Kansas & Pacific Railroad. J. Wright Mooar as well as Buffalo Bill and Pete Snyder, helped supply meat for railroad company employees. (Photo courtesy Library of Congress, Washington, D.C.)

WILLIAM HENRY "PETE" SNYDER became a friend of J. Wright Mooar while both were hunting buffalo for the railroad in Kansas. Snyder was mostly concerned with furnishing supplies for the hunters, but he and Mooar remained together, and by 1876, both had arrived in Scurry County, Texas. (Photo courtesy Colorado City Museum, Colorado City, Texas)

CHIEF DULL KNIFE OF THE NORTHERN CHEYENNE. "Pete" Snyder would always remember the Cheyenne Indians. While working for the Kansas & Pacific Railroad in 1866, he lost part of an ear during a battle with these Indians. (Photo courtesy National Archives, Washington, D.C.)

Chapter 3

Two Lawless Companions
1872

Dodge City proved to be the perfect center of trade for the new buffalo hide business. The Santa Fe Railroad had just made its way to the little frontier town, and hides were easily shipped back East. On the dark side, Dodge was also filled with lawless men, many of whom had been driven from their homes in both the North and South after the Civil War. Men of this caliber helped establish towns all along the frontier West, and Dodge City had its share of outlaws. The town became known as "Hell on the Plains."

Mooar's company continued to send caravans from Dodge City to all parts of Kansas, and it was on one of these expeditions that young Wright learned just how lawless some of these characters could be.

Mooar, along with an older man and a young boy, set out with two teams to make a new camp on the Arkansas River, and wandered along for four or five days looking for a possible site. About a hundred miles upriver they came onto an old rock house that had been a station for the Pony Express during 1860 and 1861. The house had long been abandoned, but it was quickly remodeled and would serve as their base camp. They cut and stacked enough hay to feed their horses for several days, and Wright and the old man made plans to take a load of meat to a trading post seventy-five miles away the next day. It was a long trip, but they needed supplies.

Mooar usually fell asleep quickly, especially when he had others around, but that night he sensed something was wrong. Wright got up from his bunk and stood in the door of the stone house looking across the prairie with its crescent moon hovering just over the river in the east. The howling of coyotes and wolves mingled with the wind. Everything was as it should be, even the buffalos on the hillside across the Arkansas.

Wright's mind wandered to his purpose for being in that place at that time. 'Was it worth the price one must pay?' He looked across the river at the great shaggy beasts outlined in the moonlight, and knew it was worth any price.

The man and boy were tossing gently as they slept. Wright crept back to his bunk and pulled a light buffalo robe over his feet. Nothing more was necessary for a summer night on the Kansas Plains. He lay awake listening to the spring branch on the east side of the house flowing downhill toward the Arkansas River. Its gentle murmurs blended with a thousand other night sounds.

Wright lay motionless for a long time; he did not sleep well inside a house, and usually spread his blankets underneath his wagon on the open prairie. Tonight, however, he would try to sleep in a bunk. Thoughts of his brother and the new business back in Dodge City ran through his mind. He and John had always been close and the company was becoming a success. Everyone seemed happy with the newly formed enterprise.

'This is a long way from Pownal, Vermont,' Wright thought, as he remembered his parents still living there. He listened to howls of coyotes and wolves mingling with the singing of prairie insects. A great Western frontier musical stage surrounded him as he lay in his bunk. Everything Wright had ever dreamed of was here in this land of adventure. He fell asleep thinking how different his life had become...

About two o'clock, Mooar suddenly awakened. Life on the prairie had instilled in him a sense of knowing when danger was near. He lay taut, and finally heard the sound of murmuring voices.

"It's dangerous, and I don't want to do it!" the young boy protested, fear evident in his voice.

Wright slipped from his bunk and crept to the doorway that separated the two rooms. The moon had moved across the sky, and he knew he'd been asleep for several hours; it was closer to dawn now, long after midnight. Silence gripped the still, early morning air as Wright stood motionless listening intently.

"I don't want to!" the boy protested once again.

"Sh-h-h, not so loud!" the man whispered. "He's sleepin', and there ain't gonna be no danger. During this trip, he's just gonna disappear." [1]

Fear gripped Wright, for now he knew their plan was to kill him! The two continued discussing their plot for his death.

"Nobody'll know about it for months, and then we'll tell all about how the Indians got 'im,"[2] the man argued over and over. After awhile they lowered their voices to a whisper and Wright could not hear what they were saying. He had, however, understood enough of their plot to know that they planned his murder.

The two men left their bunks and started for Wright's room. He quickly jumped back into his bunk.

"Are you awake, Wright?" the man called.

Convinced that playing 'possum was his best plan, Wright did not reply. The man called again, but Wright still did not respond. Apparently convinced that Mooar was asleep and had not heard them talking, the two went back to their own bunks.

Wright did not sleep any more that night, finally getting up and gazing out the window toward the west. The moon was falling behind the hills, and the early morning calls of coyotes and wolves echoed across the prairie. The buffalo herd on the hillside across the river was moving toward the open plains.

'It isn't a very good night for sleeping, anyway,' Wright thought to himself as his two murderous companions slumbered nearby. He had to make preparations to escape his planned fate, but decided to await daybreak to make his move. Wright Mooar had not seen enough of the West, and certainly was not ready to die...

"THE HERD OF BUFFALO across the Arkansas River was moving toward the open plains; Mooar walked to the window to watch them..." (Photo courtesy The Forest Service, National Archives, Washington, D.C.)

Chapter 4

Escape From Death
(1872)

The next three hours until daybreak were like an eternity to Wright Mooar. In his mind, he had retraced every event of the last few days. Finally, they began to fall into place. Wright realized the man had planned his death for this particular trip from the very beginning of his employment back in Dodge City.

By dawn, Mooar had carefully finalized his plans for escape. He grew more nervous as the sun peaked over the eastern hills and the two men stirred in their bunks. Soon, they were up busily preparing breakfast.

"I'm sick," Wright said. "I don't feel like eating."

"What's the matter?" the man asked, half suspecting that Wright knew something of his deadly plans.

"I'm just sick," Mooar replied as he sat down to watch the pair. The men finished their breakfast of buffalo meat, beans and coffee, and went about their morning chores. Wright wondered if they suspected he knew of their plot.

"I'm sick and I must go back to Dodge," he said firmly to the man. Wright held his rifle in his lap and added ammunition as he spoke. An expression of guilt spread across the young boy's face as he turned aside.

"I'm sorry you're sick," the man said, trying to preserve his composure. "You go on back to Dodge and me and the boy'll go on. We are sorry to lose you, but you are your own boss."[3]

Wright continued toying with his gun during the conversation. "Let's divide the supplies," he said as he stood his distance. That done, Mooar headed the team toward Dodge, all the while keeping a wary eye behind him to see if the pair was following.

Moving swiftly, Wright covered a lot of ground in a short time. His sense of fear and danger seemed to communicate itself to the mules, and they moved as quickly as possible over the Kansas plains. They soon left the old rock house far behind.

When Mooar reached the the Arkansas, he dumped the provisions into the river, fearing his treacherous companions had poisoned the food. A rainstorm upstream had caused the river to rise considerably and the murky water quickly took the provisions away.

Later that afternoon, Wright stopped long enough to kill a buffalo for meat. Cutting off a hind quarter, he moved on toward Dodge City. About sunset, he spotted a herd of cattle on the horizon and headed in that direction.

"Can I camp with you tonight?" he asked the trail boss. The cattlemen were glad to have a visitor and welcomed Wright. The cowboys' supper was already prepared, and he was asked to share the meal. "The buffalo meat can be fixed later," they told Wright, and he readily joined them.

Learning of the plot to kill him, the cowmen assured Wright Mooar that he was safe with them. That night, he slept soundly underneath his wagon, thoughts of his experience and his narrow escape soon lost in a deep sleep.

Next morning, Wright ate breakfast with the cowmen and once again headed for Dodge City. He had learned a valuable lesson, but he was not finished with buffalo hunting. He would go back to his company headquarters and ready himself for another hunt. This time, though, J. Wright Mooar would choose his hunting companions a bit more carefully...

Chapter 5

Wright Sees the Great Herd
(August, 1872)

Wright soon made his way safely to Dodge City and rejoined John and Charles who had continued the company operation while he had been away on the hunt.

By late July, Mooar had planned another expedition along the Arkansas River. Despite his harrowing experience there in June, he had come to love the area and was anxious to return. His hunting outfit arrived on the Arkansas in early August and set up camp.

One morning as he was riding south of the river, there appeared to be millions of buffalo coming up from the Texas plains. The herd stretched north to south for almost a hundred miles and Wright estimated the herd to be seven to eight miles wide.

He hunted from the herd for several days and could hardly believe his great good fortune. Later in life, he would be remembered as one of the few white men who had seen one of the great American buffalo herds.

The buffalo moved as if being led by an invisible hand. The Arkansas was on a great rise because of the summer rains, and was about seven hundred yards wide in some places. The herd came rapidly, but was slowed momentarily by the rising water. After some turmoil among themselves, the prime buffalo plunged into the swirling river and made their way quickly to the other side heading for summer grazing. Many of these animals would never return to the Arkansas River area; they would be killed by hunters on the northern plains.

As the stronger animals crossed the river, the weaker ones, mostly cows and calves, turned back toward Texas. Great clouds of dust could be seen for miles as they plowed over the prairie, and the sounds of their hooves hitting the hard Kansas soil could be heard at a great distance. The whole scene was like a miracle.

HOME OF THE BUFFALO. These giant animals roamed from Canada to Mexico before hunters killed them off in the 1860s and 1870s. By 1880, only a few bison were left. (Photo courtesy The Brininstool Collection, Amon Carter Museum, Ft. Worth, Texas)

Wright knew there must be other herds to the south, but right now, Kansas seemed to hold enough buffalo to keep him busy. After several days of taking the animals he needed, Mooar loaded his wagons and returned to Dodge City. As he drove, J. Wright Mooar wondered if anyone would believe him when he told them about having seen the great Texas buffalo herd...

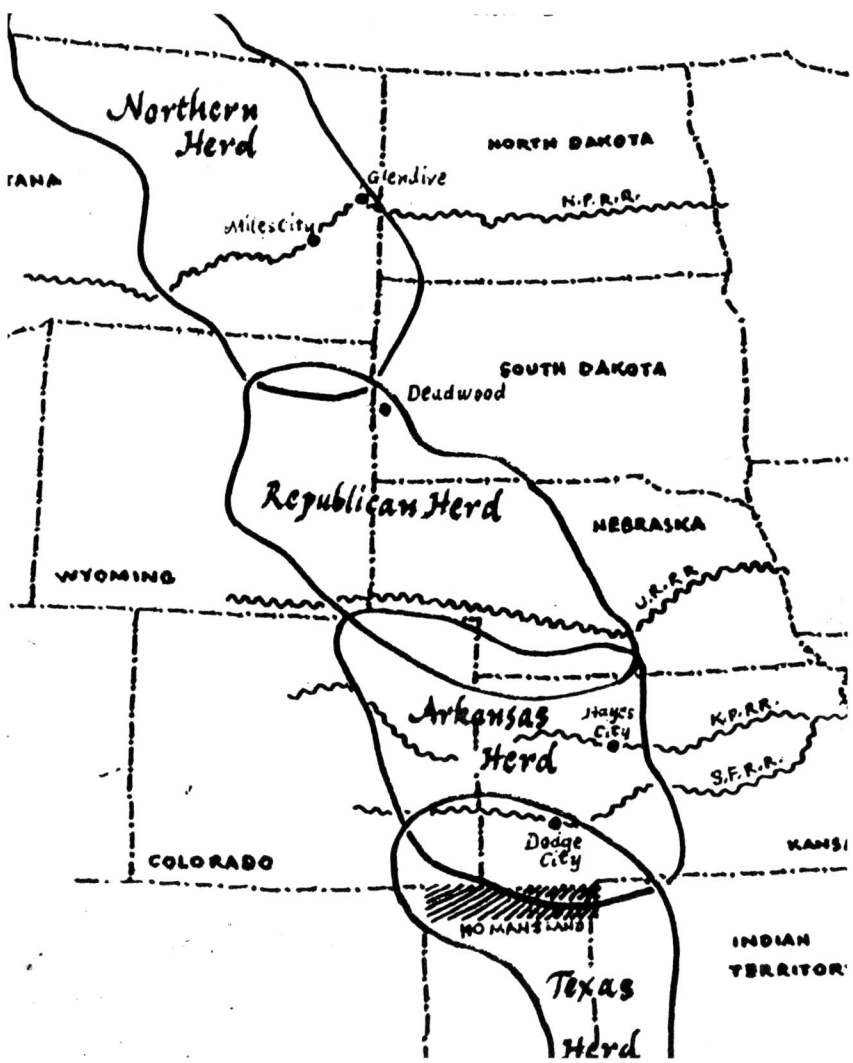

THE FOUR GREAT BUFFALO HERDS of the Great Plains - c. 1870. (Drawing from The Saga of The Buffalo, Cy Martin, Hart Publishing Co., New York, 1973)

Chapter 6

Lost In A Blizzard
(January, 1873)

The Mooar Brothers and Wright Company sent out several expeditions during the fall and winter of 1872-1873. It had been an especially harsh winter, but the hunting had been good. Buffalo grow thick hair for protection in cold weather and these hides were even more valuable.

Wright continued as the main hunter while his partners took care of the skinning and the marketing of the hides back East.

In January, 1873, Wright, John and their men were on their way back to Dodge City after a successful hunt. It had been a long and hard hunt on Kiowa Creek, about forty miles from Dodge west of Medicine Lodge. Because the winter was more severe than had been expected, the weather was beginning to take its toll on both the men and animals. They all looked forward to arriving back at their Dodge headquarters.

The wagons were loaded with hides and the poles and wrappings of their shelters; the mule teams were hitched and ready to go. The Mooars pushed the mules hard the first day and had arrived at Mulberry Creek when a 'norther' hit without warning. The men thought the storm would pass in a little while, but by late afternoon, it had gotten worse. They headed their wagons to John Hunt's cabin which was known to be nearby.

Both men and animals were blinded by blowing snow and ice, and the mules often lost their footing and slipped to the ground.

"Death stared us in the face that day," Wright recalled, remembering the terrible blizzard.

The trail was entirely lost in the storm, but the teams managed to stay together. The hunters knew the Hunt cabin was close, but they simply could not locate it. The homestead was their only chance for shelter for themselves and a barn for their animals. They searched desperately, but could not find the house in the sea of snow and ice.

Suddenly, one of the mules stopped in his tracks and the procession came to a halt. The men jumped out of their wagons to prod the mule, but found that the animal had frozen to death in his tracks! They quickly unhitched him and pushed him aside.

One of the skinners lost his sight from the blinding snow and severe cold. John cupped his hands, blew warmth into them and placed them over the man's eyes. Repeating this process several times, the man's eyesight was slowly regained.

The hunters yelled and shoved on the lead mule in a desparate effort to get her moving, but she stubbornly stood her ground. One of the drivers took a running lunge at the mule, but she turned quickly, shoving the man into the wall of a building covered in snow and ice! The mules had instinctively led them to John Hunt's cabin!

With a roaring fire for themselves and a warm stable for their animals, the Mooars and their hunters and skinners spent a more comfortable night than they had just shortly before imagined. As he snuggled before the fireplace in a buffalo robe listening to the howling blizzard outside, Wright considered the close call that had been averted...

THE MOOAR PARTY finally made its way safely into Dodge. The toll bridge across the Arkansas River was completed in 1874, shortly after the Mooars were there. This photo was taken in 1888, soon after Ford County purchased the bridge and removed the toll. (Photo courtesy Boot Hill Museum, Dodge City, Kansas)

Chapter 7

A Decision To Move... Let's Get Out Of Dodge
(Spring, 1873)

The men awoke next morning to find the prairie draped in a blanket of white as far as they could see. The snow was blinding against the clear blue sky. The wind had subsided, but it was still bitterly cold, as one could expect after a Kansas blizzard.

The men stayed at the cabin until the sun finally began to melt the snow. The teams were harnessed and they headed for Dodge. The Mooars and their party arrived safely in the town after a hard journey and spent the remainder of the winter there. The narrow escape at Kiowa Creek convinced them that it was simply too dangerous to venture that far away from Dodge to winter hunt.

Other hunting parties had made Dodge City their headquarters as well, and the Mooars realized there were simply too many outfits in the area for the dwindling herds. In 1873, Dodge had 4,000 residents, about three-fourths of whom were buffalo hunters. A great number of the remaining townsfolk were whiskey drinking hunters, many who had dodged their military service either for the North or South, and prostitutes who worked in the saloons during the day and early evening, and in the sporting houses at night. It was a town where a life was considered of little value and burials were frequent. Men hardly looked up from their card playing and whiskey drinking to see a wagon go by with a body for Boot Hill. The saloons were the most popular places in town, and churches or church services were rare.

"There are just too many people in Dodge," Wright told John. "We've got to move to another territory where there are more buffalo and fewer hunters."

Wright and John knew that hunting in Texas violated the 1867 Medicine Lodge Treaty with the Indians, so they sought the advice of Colonel (Major) Richard I. Dodge, the commander of Ft. Dodge. Besides the Indians themselves, the army was the only obstacle to prevent buffalo hunters from going into the Texas Panhandle. According to Wright, they "slicked up" and put on new clothes to approach the fort's commander.

DODGE CITY, 1872; the wagon is loaded with buffalo hides. (Photo courtesy Kansas State Historical Society, Topeka, Kansas)

NEAR EXTINCTION. Not only were the buffalo disappearing from the prairies, Indian tipis were soon to be a thing of the past as well. (Photo courtesy National Archives, Washington, D.C.)

At first the commander would not see them, but upon learning that buffalo hunters awaited an audience, he consented to an interview. After visiting with Wright and Steele Frazier, another hunter, for a while, the Colonel advised them, "If I were a buffalo hunter, I would go where the buffalo are."

This was what the hunters wanted to hear. The Mooars began immediate plans for their move into the Texas Panhandle. In the meantime, however, the Mooars would continue shorter forays around Dodge City, and as soon as their affairs were in order, move into Texas.

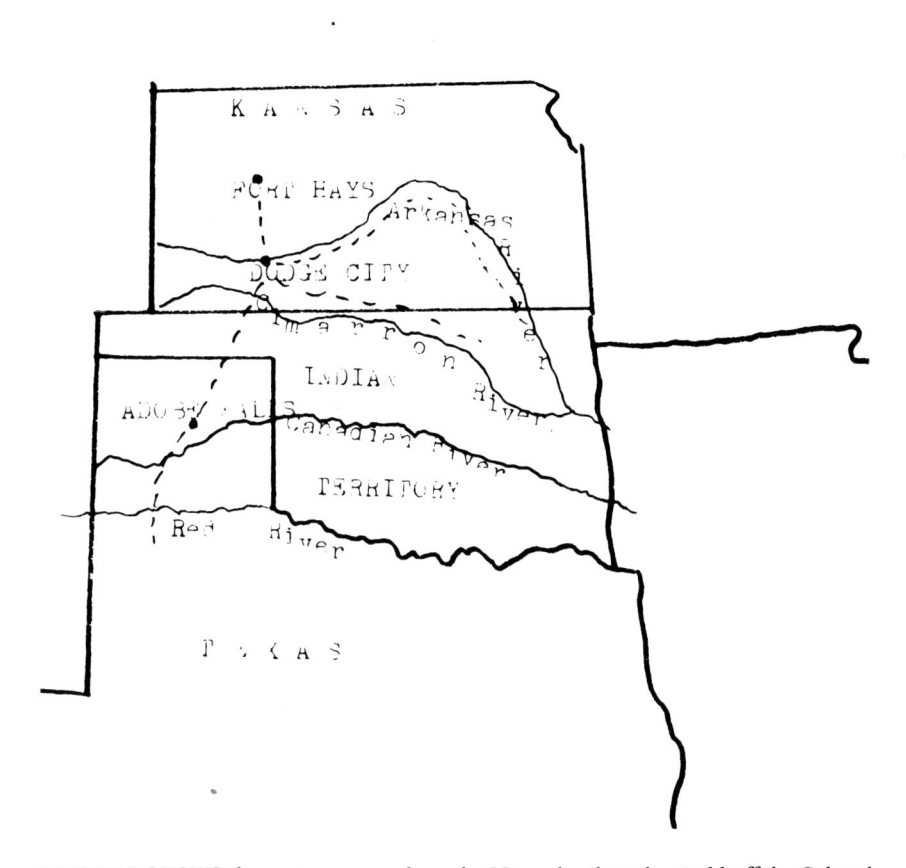

THIS MAP SHOWS the major areas where the Mooar brothers hunted buffalo. Colonel (Major) Richard Dodge, commander at Ft. Dodge told them, "If I were a buffalo hunter, I would hunt where the buffalo are." This led to an expedition into the Texas Panhandle, and a major hunt was launched by the Mooar hunters in that area in the fall of 1873 (Map drawn by Jo Laster, Union City, Tennessee)

On one of their shorter hunts in early spring, 1873, John suddenly became ill. Wright rushed him back to Dodge City where he was diagnosed as having double pneumonia. Wright sat at his bedside for six weeks while John hovered between life and death.

The move to Texas was delayed until John had regained his strength. The rest of the Mooar crew spent the time in short hunts around Dodge, but most of these forays were unsuccessful because of the large number of hunters on the Kansas Plains. The men waited patiently, but they were anxious to get away to Texas where the hunting would be better.

When John was well enough to travel, the outfit camped in the Cimarron River area to make final plans for their move south. They remained at that place throughout the summer of 1873 with other hunters who had joined together with the Mooars for protection agains the Indians. Most of the Plains Indians had been sent to reservations, but there were bands of renegades still about who had joined together against the buffalo hunters.

The men knew there was another big herd of buffalo out there, because many of them had seen the same great herd that Wright saw along the Arkansas the year before. The men generally agreed that the animals were probably somewhere in the territory controlled by the Indians through the Medicine Lodge Treaty. This territory included the Texas Panhandle with its lush canyons that provided year long grazing and protection for the bison in winter. The Panhandle was also a good place for the Indians, who knew every canyon and valley in which to hide. This area was forbidden land and Wright knew his outfit had to plan very carefully to carry off a large buffalo hunt here in the middle of Indian territory. He had heard tales of the savagery of the red men toward the white hunter who ventured into the Texas Panhandle...

The hunting crew chose Wright Mooar and John Webb to search north Texas for buffalo. In August, 1873, the men left their Cimarron camp, traveled across the North Canadian River and into the Texas Panhandle. They each took 200 rounds of ammunition, Big Fifty Sharps rifles, and salt. Mooar and Webb took the fastest horses in camp, but they weren't sure their mounts were quick enough to evade the Indians war ponies.

Occasionally, a band of Indians was seen in the distance, and small herds of buffalo were spotted on the horizon. Pushing on, the two men were soon lost in the thousands of bison grazing in the draws. As they rode farther south, the giant beasts parted to make a path for the hunters and their horses. The grass was lush and the animals were fat from spring and summer grazing. In the evening, the sun slowly set over the Texas Panhandle canyons, and buffalo shadows grew long as Mooar and Webb watched.

At night, the men slept on saddles and blankets surrounded by the great herd. While the men were not afraid of being attacked, they were cautious of a stampede and were careful to select campsites on hills or at the edges of canyons, places that could not be easily reached by stampeding buffalo. Many of the animals were yearlings born that spring. The rest of the herd were the great bulls and cows that weighed upwards of two thousand pounds. The shaggy manes of the bulls often caught in the wind and made the animals look much larger than they actually were.

Wright Mooar and John Webb rode for five days through the canyons of the Texas Panhandle. Red clay met blue sky, while the great herd of buffalo grazed the hills and lowlands on every side. The hills held dripping springs and streams ran through the bottoms of the canyons, supplying an abundance of water for the area. The Indians either had not seen them or chose not to attack the two white hunters.

On the sixth day, Mooar and Webb hurried back toward the Cimarron River to their base camp. Their crews anxiously awaited their news. The two scouts gave glowing reports of the great herd and the beautiful countryside with its plentiful water and grazing.

The hunters listened intently and were eager to begin the hunt in Texas. A treaty with the Indians was going to be broken, and the Mooar Brothers Company was among the first to enter the forbidden territory. (Charles Wright had withdrawn from the company in 1873).

Unknown to them, plenty of trouble was brewing in the Texas Panhandle. The Indians knew the hunters were coming and were waiting for them... The whites had once again betrayed the red man and the Plains Indians banded together to drive the buffalo hunters from their lands.

There would be bloodshed, and J. Wright Mooar and his outfit would be right in the middle of it...

BUFFALO ON THE GOODNIGHT RANCH. This photo, dated May 2, 1891, is of a small herd of buffalo on the huge Charlie Goodnight ranch in the Texas Panhandle. These are but a few remaining bison from the vast herds that J. Wright Mooar saw in 1873. (Photo courtesy the Amon Carter Museum, Ft. Worth, Texas)

Chapter 8

The Panhandle Expedition
Fall 1873 - Summer 1874)

In September, 1873, Wright and John Mooar with eight other hunters and four wagons, each pulled by a team of four mules, set out from their Cimarron River camp for Texas. The wagons could haul 10,000 pounds over frozen ground when they were hitched to four mules.

The outfit crossed the neutral strip (now, the Oklahoma Panhandle) between Kansas and Texas, which was supposed to serve as a barrier against buffalo hunters, and shortly made camp at Palo Duro Creek. The Medicine Lodge Treaty had been broken; there were now white men on the Indians' hunting grounds. The men found the territory everything Wright Mooar and John Webb had promised it would be, flowing streams, abundant grass and buffalo by the hundreds of thousands.

The hunters moved farther into the deep canyons, looking to flush the buffalo onto the plains. Instead, on one hunt, they flushed a group of thirty or so Comancheros, Hispanics from New Mexico who were running a contraband trade with the Indians on the Llano Estacado. The bandits, who probably hated whites more than the Plains Indians did, feared the buffalo hunters would interfere with their nefarious enterprise and repeatedly attacked the hunters. The Comancheros, however, were finally driven away by the heavy fire of the hunters' buffalo guns.

Wright said that the hunters were armed with the .50/70 Trapdoor Springfield army rifle. It shot a centerfire cartridge loaded with 70 grains of black powder and a .50 caliber "swadged ring ball." The Comancheros and Indians had obtained rifles of lighter calibers in trade with other bandits, but the buffalo hunters' guns were extremely accurate at much longer distances.

The Mooars and their company were hunting about seven miles from an outfit that belonged to Lane and Wheeler. The two parties checked on one another throughout each day by listening for the heavy booming of the buffalo guns. They knew the difference in the sound of gunfire from the lighter rifles of the Indians and that of the buffalo hunters' guns. If they didn't hear them, a party would ride the distance to check on the other. Wheeler had not found the number of buffalo he needed to fill the 10,000-pound capacity of his outfit's wagons, and without telling the Mooars, had moved on to the precarious Canadian River area.

Wheeler was wounded during an Indian attack after he had hit one of the warriors with a blacksnake whip. Against Wright's advice, Wheeler's brother took him back to Dodge City, where he died shortly thereafter.

* * *

In March, 1874, Charlie Myers, a Dodge City dealer in buffalo hides and hunter supplies, set up a branch store on the Canadian River with Fred Leonard as clerk; he called it Adobe Walls for the old abandoned post a few miles upriver, built by the Bents for their trade with the Plains Indians almost 30 years before. Attached to his store, Myers built a large stockaded corral with a storehouse in one corner. He soon had competition from Charlie Rath, another trader from Dodge, who built a sod store, and from Jim Hanrahan who threw up a sod saloon nearby. When Myers brought in $50,000 in goods, Rath brought in $20,000 worth. Shortly, Tom O'Keefe erected a picket and post blacksmith shop between Myers' and Hanrahan's. Adobe Walls was soon the headquarters for the buffalo hunters in the Texas Panhandle.

Whether for protection or just coincidence, the outpost was built in the middle of a prairie dog colony. This situation would prove of some value later.

The Mooars continued hunting in this area, but decided to move their base of operations to Adobe Walls for its protection against the hostile Indians. John was kept busy taking loads of buffalo hides into Dodge and returning to Adobe Walls with supplies for Myers' store. Wright was more interested in hunting than hauling, and although John hunted too, he liked this arrangement just as well. The Mooars kept this campsite through the winter of 1873 and into the summer of 1874.

In early May, 1874, Wright and five hunting companions set out from Adobe Walls to hunt near Red Deer Creek. A couple of their fellow hunters, Dave Dudley and Tommy Wallace, who had been hunting that area, were caught in camp by raiding Indians. They killed both hunters and drove a stake through Dudley's abdomen into the ground, and mutilated him. John Thomson Jones (also called "Anteope Jack" or "Cheyenne Jack") and W. Muhler ("Blue

Billy") were also killed near Red Deer Creek.

Regardless of the danger, Wright and his friends traveled up the canyons and into the valleys to hunt. They made their camp near the creek, circling the wagons at night with their animals and themselves inside.

While camped there one evening, a band of Indians came near and sat mounted on their horses a short distance away. Wright walked out toward them and motioned for them to come into camp. The Indians in feathers and war paint, sat motionless, then upon a command from their leader, they vanished behind a hill.

Fearing the Indians would attack during the night, Wright told the hunters to pull up camp. They moved several miles up the creek and set up in an open area which seemed safe from an ambush. Buffalo hunters did not like to camp near timber or the river unless it was absolutely necessary.

WARRIORS OF THE PLAINS. (Photo courtesy Cy Martin, Saga of the Buffalo, Hart Publishing Co., New York, 1973)

"We'd better post guards tonight," Wright told the men.

Each man took a turn at guard duty that night. Every sound was mistaken for an Indian attack, but the night dragged on without further incident. The moon hung lazily in the sky as the men slumbered, but long before the sun peeked over the Texas hills, the men rose. At dawn, the Indians attacked. The wagons had been pulled into a circle, and Wright Mooar had been sleeping with his Big Fifty Sharps under a blanket near his bedroll.

Some of the outfit's animals were grazing a short distance from camp; Lemnot (Lem) Wilson and Phillip Sisk ran to bring them into the safety of the circled wagons.

The Indians yelled as they raced toward the buffalo hunters. Wright aimed at the lead Indian who was hanging onto the opposite side of his horse shooting from beneath the animal's neck. A .50 caliber ball from the big buffalo gun tore through both horse and rider. The Indians apparently had not seen such a rifle, for they were stunned by its effectiveness.

The buffalo hunters kept up a steady fire, and the Indians retreated to cover in some brush a short distance away. The muzzle blasts from their smaller rifles could be seen in the early morning light, and every shot was answered with a volley from the big buffalo guns. These rifles could kill a bull buffalo at six hundred yards and the balls shot from the rifles could tear away the leg of a horse or man on impact. The Big Fifty Sharps Rifle was the most popular gun of the times, having been made especially for buffalo hunting.

The Indians were furious at the destruction from the guns of the hunters. Two of the warriors, still hanging onto the sides of their horses, made another dash toward the circled wagons. Somehow escaping the fire from the hunters, the men made two or three unsuccessful attempts to kill the hunters. Finally, under a barrage of bullets, they recovered two of their fallen warriors and returned to their comrades. The band quickly rode away into the early morning dawn, and were not seen again that day.

Wright had heard reports that hundreds of Indians were leaving the reservations to help drive the buffalo hunters from their territory. He realized, too, that the outpost at Adobe Walls would come in for its share of Indian attacks, and he was anxious to return there. From Adobe Walls, he and John would transport the hides back to Dodge City.

There were too many hides at the Red Deer Creek camp for the equipment they had with them. Wright sent one of the men to Adobe Walls to bring John and more wagons.

BUFFALO HIDES IN DODGE CITY. Stacked in Rath & Wright's hide yard, 40,000 buffalo hides are ready for shipment by train to the East. D.W. Anchutz (in the white shirt, rear of photo) ran the hide press for the company. Charlie Rath himself sits atop the pile of buff hides at the right. (Photo courtesy Kansas State Historical Society, Topeka, Kansas).

Chapter 9

Unrest At Adobe Walls
(June, 1874)

Wright's messenger rode into the Walls just as John Mooar drove his team in from a delivery to Dodge City. The supplies were a welcome sight for the inhabitants, and they were anxious to hear news from Dodge.

John made hasty preparations for the journey to Red Deer Creek after learning of the Indian attack. Just as the wagons were ready for the trip, an army sergeant, four soldiers and a government scout rode into camp. The group looked suspicious and the camp was further excited by their appearance.

The hunters questioned the group closely; the soldiers said they were looking for horse thieves. Amos Chapman, the half breed scout, remained in the background as the hunters pumped the soldiers with questions. "You came to the wrong place, mister!" shouted one of the hunters angrily. "We ain't used to being accused of stealing horses!" The soldiers turned and rode away a few yards where they set up their own camp. Chapman followed along, and shortly, the soldiers rode away up the river leaving the scout in charge of the camp.

"We'll be back in the morning," they shouted at Amos as they rode away.

Several of the hunters yelled threats at Amos, who was alone in the soldiers' camp. "The only good Injun is a dead one!" they shouted. News of impending Indian attacks on buffalo hunters had raised everyone's degree of hostility. The scout was alarmed, and asked to talk to the leaders at Adobe Walls. The men agreed to talk with him, and afterwards Amos refused to tell the hunters what he and the camp leaders spoke of in secret.

Every town and trading post in the West had a saloon and Adobe Walls was no different. Later in the day, the hunters had been drinking heavily at Hanrahan's and threatened to hang Chapman. Many of them had been parties to hangings before and would not hesitate to do so again.

By nightfall, plans for the lynching were well formulated. The leader of the vigilantes approached Hanrahan and confided the plans for Chapman's demise that night.

"I guess he's got it coming," Hanrahan replied, not daring to divulge the half breed's real purpose for being at the trading post. Amos had told Hanrahan and the other hunter leaders the exact date and time that Quanah Parker and his Indians would attack Adobe Walls.*

This group dared not reveal the Indians' plans for fear the hunters and skinners would flee, leaving the store owners without the protection of the big buffalo guns. Hanrahan and the others knew they were obliged to save the half-breed's life, and he immediately began his scheme.

When the vigilante told Hanrahan that they would grab Chapman in the saloon that night, he nodded as if in approval. When darkness came, Amos entered the saloon and Hanrahan took him aside before the hunters arrived for their nightly drinking spree.

WAGONS OF BUFFALO HUNTERS. This is a typical scene of the hunters and their wagons. This photo was made at Buffalo Gap, near Abilene, Texas, c. 1878. These wagons are pulled by giant oxen; one wagon is already loaded with buffalo hides. (Photo courtesy Scurry County Museum, Snyder, Texas)

*J.Wright Mooar claimed until his death that Quanah Parker sent Amos Chapman to warn the Mooars. Parker admired the brothers for their hunting skills and wanted them out of Adobe Walls before the battle. Mooar and Parker became friends later in life. Mooar related this information to his granddaughter, Judy Hays, and to many other Scurry County residents before his death.

"See that wagon over there," pointing as he spoke; Amos nodded.

"That's John Mooar's wagon. You get in it with John as soon as you leave here tonight."

Amos smiled, walked over to the bar and ordered a drink.

"I'm going out for a while to visit friends," he announced loudly. "I'll be back later to drink some more, then to sleep."

"All right, " Hanrahan called to Amos as he left the building. "We'll see you in a little while."

The bartender, who had been alerted for trouble, began his part of the scheme to save Chapman.

"Drinks on the house!" he called.

The hunters rushed the bar as Amos quickly sped away in the dark toward John Mooar's wagon.

"What are you doing here?" John questioned in surprise. Chapman did some fast talking. He told John how some of their friends had sent him to Adobe Walls to warn of the impending attack by Quanah Parker and his warriors.

"They plan to massacre everyone in the area, and we were sent to warn the hunters at Adobe Walls," Amos related.

John still had doubts about the man, but gave him protection for the night. Outside the wagon, the drunken vigilantes were heard searching. Several tripped and fell as they stepped into the prairie dog holes around the trading post.

Amos soon fell asleep, but John remained wide awake. He was thinking of his trip the next morning to Red Deer Creek and wondered what he would find there. Before the vigilantes awakened from their ordeal of the previous night, John, with three wagons and drivers, was on his way to help Wright and the party on Red Deer Creek.

Chapman slept in the back of the wagon. 'He'll be safe there for a while,' John thought as he hurried his team along toward his brother and his hunters. John wanted to be at Red Deer Creek before the Indians attacked that camp again.

Chapter 10

Fast Trip To Red Deer Creek
(June, 1874)

John drove his mule team much harder than usual, and after traveling day and night, they arrived at Wright's camp on Red Deer Creek two days later.

"The Indians are going to storm Adobe Walls," John told Wright.

"I think everyone has expected it for some time," Wright replied, seeming not the least bit surprised at the news.

The party lost no time in loading the wagons for the return trip to Adobe Walls. Rumors of Indian attacks had reached all parts of the Texas Panhandle, and hunters from everywhere were rushing to the trading post for safety.

The second day after leaving Red Deer Creek, the hunters were hit with a torrential rainstorm. The horses and mules became very nervous as heavy thunder and lightening forced the hunters to make camp at the mouth of Red Deer Creek. Two lakes served as protection against whatever dangers might lurk nearby.

The animals were staked out near the lakes for grazing. The storm clouds had dwindled somewhat, but the sky was still an overcast dull gray. A few buffalo were seen grazing on the distant flatland near the northern end of the larger lake.

Some of the men were finishing their noon meal while others dozed under the wagons. Everybody was tired from the forced travel, and a few minutes rest was welcome before continuing the journey to Adobe Walls.

Suddenly, the sound of a bugle in the distance, coming from the hunters' back trail, broke the midday silence. Wright climbed atop a wagon for a better look and saw a band of Indians rushing directly toward them at full gallop. A big, battle-ready brave in war paint, blowing the bugle, rode at the front of the Indians.

Wright jumped from the wagon and rushed for his buffalo rifle, yelling for the others to herd the horses and mules into the safety of the circled wagons.

Lem Wilson, one of John's drivers, ran across the pasture for the stock.

"Is your gun ready, Mooar?"[5] Lem yelled as he ran.

"I'm ready with forty rounds," Wright shouted back.

"Well, hold 'em back while we get the stock!" Lem urged.

Dropping to one knee to steady the fifteen pound Sharps rifle, Wright sent a .50 caliber ball screaming into the front line of the racing Indians. The lead horse jerked to one side and some of the braves stopped suddenly in confusion.

Bullet after bullet was sent into the mass of redskins and several fell from their horses. Some of them could be seen running on foot from the mass of bareback riders. The attack stopped temporarily as the Indian bugler rode around furiously trying to rally his warriors for another attack. But, they found it impossible to make advances against the heavy bombardment from the big Sharps buffalo guns. Their own light rifles could not reach the hunters from such long distances as they were forced to maintain in the face of such deadly gun fire from the buffalo hunters.

The Indians chose to withdraw.

By this time, Lem Wilson had rounded up most of the stock animals, and the hunters were desperately trying to hitch the teams to their wagons. Some of the animals broke loose in the confusion, but they were soon recovered.

Finally, the mules were hitched and the drivers headed for a crossing on the Red Deer about a mile away. They reached the ford and crossed just as a bolt of lightening shattered a dark cloud right above them. The party took refuge in a large cottonwood grove, and another great downpour drenched the hunters.

From their view, they saw heavy cloud formations farther up the creek, and within minutes, a wall of water rushed downstream, overflowed Red Deer Creek and quickly spread out onto the flatlands nearby.

Wright could see the band of Indians on the opposite bank looking at the hunters. Never had so much water been so welcome to the hunters as the lake that had been formed by the sudden cloudburst. After the rains stopped, the men took the most direct route to Adobe Walls.

Crossing the Canadian River on the third day, they set up camp in mid afternoon. While enjoying a late lunch, another band of Indians suddenly rode into camp and destroyed some of the hunters' equipment. The red men rode out as suddenly as they had arrived, though, and not a shot was fired by anyone!

"A good time was had by all, " quipped Wright later, when he learned that nobody had been hurt. Indians raided periodically during the next day, and the beleaguered hunters arrived at Adobe Walls at the end of four days from Red Deer Creek. The men had heard several reports of men behing killed in outlying areas around the trading post.

THE BODY OF A BUFFALO HUNTER, killed and scalped near Ft. Dodge, Kansas, c. 1869. (Photo courtesy Wm. Soule Collection in the Western History Collections, University of Oklahoma Library)

The whole outpost was uneasy, but very few knew that Quanah Parker with over 800 braves had already chosen the exact time for his attack on Adobe Walls. The war party was made up of braves from the Arapaho, Cheyenne, Kiowa, Comanche and other plains tribes, and were meeting at that very moment to plan the destruction of the trading post and all its inhabitants.

The battle for Adobe Walls was about to begin; buffalo hunting history would be written there on June 27, 1874...

Chapter 11

The Battle of Adobe Walls
(June 27, 1874)

The June weather brought almost unbearable heat to the Texas Panhandle, and Wright was anxious to leave Adobe Walls as early in the morning as possible. Good time could be made before the hot summer sun beat down upon them.

They knew, too, that the expected Indian attack would come

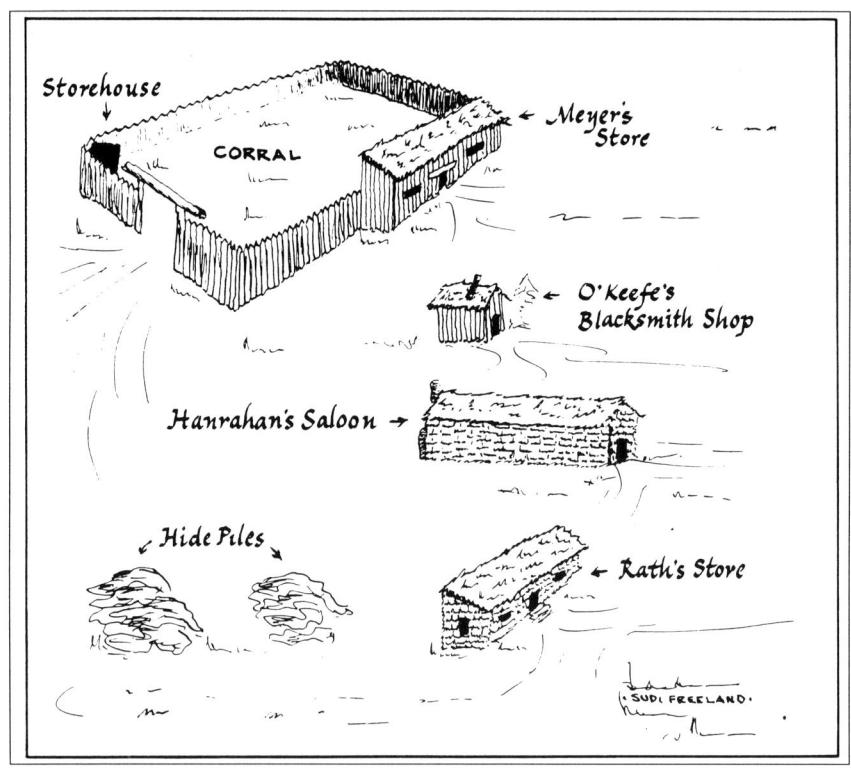

ADOBE WALLS COMPOUND, JUNE 27, 1874. (From The Saga of the Buffalo by Cy Martin; drawn by Sudi Freeland, 1973).

soon and wanted to get their shipment of hides to Dodge City as quickly as possible. Amos Chapman had told Wright's outfit the whole story of the planned attack by Quanah Parker, and had left the hunters at Red Deer Creek, opting not to return to Adobe Walls and its lynch mob vigilantes.

"We're leaving, too," Wright told John when they arrived at the trading post. The next morning at dawn*, the Mooars headed their teams toward Dodge City. About eight miles out from Adobe Walls, they ran into C.E. "Dirty Face" Jones, a friend and hunter from Dodge. He was a likable fellow, even though he never washed the dirt and tobacco juice from his face; hence, his nickname.

"You shouldn't go to the post," Wright warned Jones.

"I've got a load of ammunition for them," Dirty Face replied, "but I'll catch up with you later."

Jones then made a prophecy of certain men being killed at Adobe Walls and headed his team of six mules toward the outpost. John and Wright chuckled at Dirty Face's prophecy and drove on toward Dodge City.

Jones arrived at Adobe Walls, unloaded his wagon of ammunition, reloaded with buffalo hides, slept five hours and caught the Mooar's outfit the next day at Palo Duro Creek. The caravan made its way into Dodge on the evening of June 29. Shortly, news

*Mooar stated no specific date, but most historians give the date as June 11.

LIST OF ADOBE WALLS DEFENDERS

James Hanrahan
Bat Masterson
Mike Welch
Will Shepherd
Hiram Watson
Billy Ogg
James McKinley
"Bermuda" Jim Carlisle
William Dixon
Fred Leonard
James Campbell
Edward Trevor
Frank Brown
Charlie (Harry) Armitage

*Billy Tyler
"Dutch" Henry Born
Old Man Keeler
Mike McCabe
Henry Lease
"Frenchy"
James Langton
George Eddy
Thomas O'Keefe
*William Olds
Sam Smith
Andrew Johnson
*Ike Shadler
*"Shorty" Shadler

Mrs. William (Hannah) Olds

of the battle of Adobe Walls reached them, and they learned that most of Dirty Face Jones' prophecy had been fulfilled; some of the names he had given the Mooars on the trail, had been killed* during the Indian raid on Adobe Walls on June 27, 1874...

Wright heard later that the outpost had been defended by twenty-eight men and one woman. The Indians numbered between eight and twelve hundred, braves led by half breed Comanche Chief Quanah Parker. Although his mother was a white woman, Cynthia Ann Parker, kidnapped from her home in Texas when she was nine years old, Parker hated the whites who were bringing death and destruction to his lands, his livelihood and his red brethern.

Parker chose the bravest warriors from the Comanche, Cheyenne, Arapaho and Kiowa tribes, and they were determined to kill every hunter who had broken the Medicine Lodge Treaty. The men at the outpost who knew of the plan dared not tell the rest for fear the place would be left relatively unarmed. It is known that James Hanrahan, the saloon owner, knew of the intended Indian attack and kept the information to himself. Pretending that the ridge pole of the saloon was about to fall, he awoke the hunters in the early hours of the morning for help. Hanrahan's plan for alerting the men to impending danger had worked. The men gathered at the bar when drinks were offered, but unknown to the men inside Hanrahan's saloon, Quanah Parker and his huge war party were riding toward Adobe Walls. They were not in a hurry; the time for their attack had not yet arrived. When the time was right, the Indians would be ready and in place ...

Chief Parker stopped occasionally in the setting summer moon [6] to listen to Isatai, the Comanche medicine man, forecast death for the white men at the trading post. Parker had learned enough of the ways of the whites to put little faith in a medicine man, but he was willing to go along with the old Indian ways if it would help rid them of the intruders.

---

*Billy Dixon, one of the Adobe Walls defenders, stood thunderstruck when the attack came. He later stated he thought the Indians were just coming for the hunters' horses and mules. He soon realized, though, that they were headed straight for him and his scalp! Men, many of them still reeling from the previous night's drinking bout and some only in their underwear, ran in every direction trying to reach their rifles.

Billy Tyler was wounded as he ran to get the horses. Bat Masterson, Tyler's friend, rushed outside and brought Billy back into the store, but he died soon afterwards. Ike and "Shorty" Shadler were also killed.

This monument on the site of the 1874 Battle of Adobe Walls, was erected on the 50th Anniversary of the battle by the Panhandle Plains Historical Society, under the direction of Mrs. Billy Dixon and James H. Cator. The land for the monument was donated to the historical society by Mr. & Mrs. W.T. Coble, and is on The Turkey Track Ranch, Hutchinson County, Texas. (Photo courtesy Butch Winter, Union City, Tennessee)

William Olds was accidentally killed when his gun went off and shot him in the head. Olds and his wife were just opening a restaurant in the rear of Rath and Wright's store (managed by James Langton) when the attack began. The men did not want the Indians to know a white woman was among the defenders as they often made slaves of their white female captives and usually physically abused them severely. Knowledge that Olds' wife was in Adobe Walls would have spurred the Indians' efforts to capture the outpost.

The Shadler brothers had just brought in a load of supplies from Dodge and had planned to return with a load of hides. They were still asleep in the wagon when the Indians attacked. Both men were killed and scalped, and left sprawling face up near their wagons. Their black Newfoundland dog put up a fight, but was also killed, and one of the Indians took a giant swath of hair from his side which was seen waving from a lance during the battle.

Langton had cut sod squares and built a tower on the roof of the store just tall enough for a man to stand with head and shoulders sticking out the top. The other defenders had also cut holes in the sod roofs and were standing guard as well. The afternoon of July 2, William Olds was in the tower when another Indian attack began.

Olds started down the ladder carrying his gun butt down. He jumped from the ladder, the gun butt struck the floor and fired, sending a bullet through his head which blew the entire top away. After the attack, Olds was buried in a hastily dug grave sixty feet southeast of Rath's store.*

*Ref: Rath, Ida Ellen, *The Rath Trail*, McCormick-Armstrong, Wichita, 1961, p. 116

VIEW FROM THE ADOBE WALLS MEMORIAL. Facing east; the memorial sits on the site of the original Adobe Walls fight. This is the buffalo country which so enthralled the hunters. The butte on the left is where Billy Dixon shot the Indian from his horse 1,538 yards away. (Photo courtesy Sharon Cunningham, Union City, Tennessee).

PROTECTED SITE. The area surrounding the Adobe Walls site is a State of Texas protected archeological dig. (Photo courtesy Butch Winter, Union City, Tennessee).

ADOBE WALLS MEMORIAL. Looking west; the memorial sits in a valley that runs northeast/southwest between low butte-type hills. (Photo courtesy Sharon Cunningham, Union City, Tennessee).

CHIEF QUANAH PARKER. He had a white mother and a Kwahadi Comanche war chief father, Peta Nocona, and was raised among the Comanches. Quanah never gave up his Indian heritage. He hunted buffalo in Deep Creek in 1876-1877, the same years that the Mooars came there to hunt. After rampaging throughout the countryside for several years, all the Plains Indians had been rounded up and returned to reservations in Oklahoma. Parker is shown here in full war bonnet sitting on his war horse (note the tied tail) outside his tipi. (Photo courtesy Smithsonian Institution, National Anthropological Archives, Washington, D.C.)

LONE WOLF (GUI-PAH-GO), a Kiowa chief, was known throughout the Texas Panhandle area during the 1860s and 1870s. Lone Wolf was one of the primary Kiowa leaders during the Red River Indian Uprising, which began with the siege at Adobe Walls in June, 1874. This photo was taken sometime between 1868-1874. (Photo courtesy National Archives, Washington, D.C.

WHITE HORSE, TSEN-TAIN-TE, KIOWA SUB CHIEF. Indians were fighting all over Texas to protect and retain their way of nomadic life. White Horse led the attack and massacre at Howard's Wells (near Ft. Clark), Texas in 1873. (Photo courtesy National Archives, Washington, D.C.)

Arriving at Adobe Walls just as the moon was dying in the West, the Indians made their final plans for the assault on the outpost. Every warrior carried in his blood the hate of his people for the white hunters. Each had seen the death of the buffalo herds and smelled rotting buffalo flesh spread its stench across the prairies. The Medicine Lodge Treaty had promised that this would not happen... but, it had. The Plains Indians would withhold their hate for the whites no longer.

At daybreak, the Indians attacked. Shattering the morning air with blood-curdling screams, the warriors rushed the post and killed several men. Their horses stumbled in the holes of the prairie dog colony and fell to the ground. The hunters, along with one woman, Mrs. William Olds, fought bravely. They stood their ground and the Indians momentarily fell back.

The big slugs from the buffalo rifles sent several horses reeling from beneath their riders. Chief Parker and another brave climbed upon one of the buildings and punched holes in the sod roof to shoot through. They quickly retreated when the hunters began shooting through the roof at them.*

Suddenly, the sound of a bugle cracked the morning air as a mysterious Negro rider circled the outpost. The sound seemed to inspire the Indians to greater effort and as warriors were knocked from their horses by the hunters fire, their comrades rushed forward and pulled them onto their own mounts.

"I'll get that double-crossing bugler," one of the defenders declared as he aimed at the black man. A shot rang out and the Negro fell from his horse.** He lay still for only a moment, then several braves rushed into the thick of the battle to pull him away.

No one ever knew who he was, or why he had joined the Indians, but it was suspected that he had been a deserter from the U.S. Army. Quanah Parker personally led the battle, and when he was wounded early in the fighting, the Indians drew back for a while.

Later, under cover of darkness, and on orders from the outpost's leaders, Henry Lease slipped out of Adobe Walls headed to Dodge for help. Two others went to warn nearby camps. Fearing

---

*Ref: Brown, Dee, *Bury My Heart at Wounded Knee*, p. 266: "I got up on the adobe house with another Comanche," Quanah said. "We poked holes through roof to shoot."

**According to "The Adventures of A Buffalo Hunter," by Seth Hathaway, *Hunter's Frontier Times*, December, 1931, p. 133, the shooter was "Dutch Henry" Born. T. L. Baker & B. R. Harrison in *Adobe Walls, The History and Archeology of the 1874 Trading Post*, p. 76, however, state that Charley Armitage (aka Harry) was shooter of the bugler.

attacks, these hunters rushed to Adobe Walls to help in the outpost's defense. With their arrival, Quanah Parker's war party took a second look at subsequent attacks and already feeling the sting of defeat, returned to their sanctuary in Palo Duro Canyon.

The war party, venting its rage and blaming Isatai for their failure at Adobe Walls, flogged the Comanche medicine man and would have killed him but for the intervention of Quanah Parker.

Most of the hunters stayed around Adobe Walls throughout July and August, but soon drifted back to Dodge City. By late September, the men and supplies were gone from the outpost on the Canadian; soon, the Indians moved in and razed all the buildings.

The battle of Adobe Walls was over, but it was a short lived reprieve for the Plains Indians. Many buffalo hunters returned to the Panhandle for another crack at the great Texas buffalo herd, Wright Mooar among them.

INDIANS KILLED AT THE BATTLE OF ADOBE WALLS

CHEYENNES	COMANCHES
Chief-Stone-Cav-Son	Wild- Horse
Serpent-Scales	So-Ta-Do
Spotted-Feather	Best-Son-In-Law
Horse-Chief	Wolf-Tongue
Coyote	Slue-Foot
Stone-Teeth	Cheyenne
Soft-Foot	

(Names on the Indian Monument near that of the white defenders, on the site of Adobe Walls in Hutchinson County, Texas. The Indian names are published as they are chisled on the monument, which was dedicated on October 19, 1941).

THE COMANCHES. Half breed Chief Quanah Parker, who was reared an Indian in a Kwahadi nomadic camp by his white mother and war chief father, Peta Nocona, never gave up his Indian heritage. This photo is of Isa-tai (standing left), Quanah Parker (seated right), Black Horse (standing right) and Wild Horse (seated left). (Photo courtesy Smithsonian Institution, National Anthropological Archives, Washington, D.C.)

Chapter 12

**Back To Dodge City
(1874-1875)**

The Mooars stayed in Dodge for a while. Later, Wright and his outfit returned to the Cimarron area where they located a small herd and killed about four hundred buffalo.

As they were loading the hides, a howling sand storm struck and delayed the party for some time. Another party of the Mooar's drivers, coming upon Wright's bunch at Mulberry Creek, told Mooar that he and his outfit had been followed by Indians for some time.

Wright spent the winter of 1874 in Dodge City, and hunted out of his headquarters there through 1875. He found the buffalo even more scarce than the year before, as the Indians in the area were also learning. The red man was becoming even more hostile to the white hunters.

GRAVE OF WILLIAM OLDS, Adobe Walls defender who was accidentally killed on July 2, 1874, during Quanah Parker's intermittent attacks on the trading post in late June-early July. Olds' grave is on the Turkey Track Ranch in Hutchinson County, Texas. (Photo courtesy Butch Winter, Union City, Tennessee).

Few hunters ventured back into the Texas Panhandle over the next two to three years. The Indians made Palo Duro Canyon their sanctuary and dared the whites to enter the territory again.

After General Miles' 1874-1875 excursion into the area in search of hostiles, many of the renegades returned to their reservations. By summer, 1875, most of the major Indian leaders, including Quanah Parker, Wild Horse, Lone Wolf, and others, were back in captivity. Most were content to spend the remainder of their lives on reservations, but a few of these Indians simply would not - could not - conform to reservation life. They would not stay there long...

Wright Mooar eventually became friends with several of his former enemies, one of whom was Whirlwind, a Cheyenne chief. Wright hunted buffalo during the fall of 1875 and early spring of 1876, then set out to visit Whirlwind at his reservation in Indian Territory...

GENERAL NELSON MILES and Buffalo Bill. Miles (2nd left) and Buffalo Bill (left) with two scouts, view a hostile Indian camp near Pine Ridge, South Dakota on Jan. 16, 1891. Miles stalked the Indians in the Texas Panhandle to protect hunters like J. Wright Mooar. Buffalo Bill was working in Kansas when Mooar was supplying meat for the railroads. This photo was made - and copyrighted - by photographer Grabill of Deadwood, South Dakota. (Photo courtesy National Archives, Washington, DC).

Chapter 13

Chief Whirlwind
(Spring, 1876)

Wright Mooar took 450 buffalo hides to the Cheyenne at their agency in Indian Territory and paid them for a special tanning process. The hides were then shipped to the Eastern markets. Wright and Chief Whirlwind became friends, and he found his stay with the Cheyenne very pleasant.

Mooar, traveling across Kansas toward Indian Territory, noticed changes that had occured since his arrival in 1870. He saw scattered herds of buffalo, but nothing at all like those he remembered from just six years earlier. The railroad had come and the tracks seemed to have cut the wide open prairies into slices. Wright thought the land looked odd and very different, and he longed for the days when buffalo dotted the prairie grasslands.

Mooar and Whirlwind sat around the fire in the chief's tipi and talked of the old days. There was a sadness in the Cheyenne's eyes as he told about the Kiowa Chiefs Satanta and Big Tree, being shackled in irons and placed in the guard house there at the Cheyenne Agency (on their way back to prison at Huntsville, Texas; the two had been a part of the Warren Wagontrain massacre in 1871, were sentenced to life imprisonment, but were released on parole in 1873. Both had taken part in the Red River War in 1874 and were being returned to prison in Texas for breaking their paroles).

The two men talked late into the night.

"Now, it is all gone," the Cheyenne told Wright. "No buffalo to hunt now,"

"Not completely," said Mooar. "There are still buffalo in Texas."

"That soon be gone, too," Whirlwind stated, "Just wait, see."

"Some Indians are still leaving the reservations and ruining all chances for peace," Wright said.

"Fools!" the Cheyenne chief replied, "Fighting days must end."

They sat, silently looking into the fire for awhile. Neither spoke for several minutes.

Then Wright asked, "Do you know about Adobe Walls?"

CHEYENNE CHIEF WHIRLWIND. "There was sadness in Whirlwind's eyes as he spoke of Satanta and Big Tree..." This photo was taken in 1877, shortly after Wright Mooar visited the Cheyenne Agency in Indian Territory. The photographer is not recorded, but it is thought to be Wm. H. Jackson. (Photo courtesy Smithsonian Institution, National Anthropological Archives, Washington, D.C.)

Chief Whirlwind looked up and grinned. "Me there! Me help lead the battle."

"How many Indians were there," Wright asked.

"Many," the chief replied, "more than twelve hundred."[7]

"How many died?" the buffalo hunter wanted to know.

Whirlwind said that over one hundred Indians had died in the clash. They did not talk any more for awhile. The early morning sounds of the coyotes echoed across the prairie. Slumbering sounds were audible in the adjoining tipis, and the movement of horses was heard as they grazed in the fenced pasture nearby.

The two friends sat for twenty minutes or more without speaking. Finally, Wright broke the long silence.

"You got whipped pretty badly, didn't you?"

The chief answered scornfully, "Isatai, Comanche medicine man, no good. Cheyenne medicine man much better."

Whirlwind then told Mooar how the Cheyenne attacked Isatai and would have killed him if Quanah Parker had not stopped them.

"What did you do after the battle?" Wright asked.

"We go back into the canyon [Palo Duro] to live," the Indian said. "Much good hunting there until General Miles chase us."

Whirlwind laughed.

"What happened then," asked Wright.

"Me lead 'em 'long trail, round and round through Palo Duro Canyon!", the chief said.

"Did the general fall into any traps?"

Whirlwind rolled in laughter. "Humph, General Heap Big Bull.[8] We go round and round and Miles follow!"

He told Mooar how his braves led the soldiers down into the narrow canyons where there was only gyp water to drink.

"Soldiers get sick on bad water. Throw up!" he continued as he motioned with his hands to show how the soldiers held their stomachs and were sick.

"What did you do then?" Wright asked.

"Braves get on bluff and throw rocks and sticks on sick soldiers. They too sick to move." The chief roared with laughter as he told the story. "But, we no kill," Whirlwind assured Wright. "Washington army come with big gun. We 'fraid of big gun if we kill."

"What big gun?" Mooar questioned.

"General Miles bring big gun, and he shoot every sundown. BOOM! BOOM!" The chief motioned with his hands to show the gun making a big sound.

GENERAL NELSON A. MILES. He and his soldiers chased the Indians into Palo Duro Canyon after the Battle of Adobe Walls. According to Cheyenne Chief Whirlwind, the Indians laughed at the soldiers and called Miles "Heap Big Bull." (Photo courtesy Amon Carter Museum, Ft. Worth, Texas)

CHEYENNE AGENCY

"Every morning," he continued, "same gun go BOOM! BOOM!"

Mooar knew he was speaking of a cannon. Whirlwind talked more and Wright listened.

"Big gun tell Indian for fifty miles soldiers still around," the chief laughed. "But, we no fool with man with big gun. Me not fight white man again," Chief Whirlwind promised.

It was getting late and both men agreed it was time for bed.

"We talk more in morning," Whirlwind told Mooar. Opening the flap of his tipi, Whirlwind escorted Wright to his sleeping quarters nearby.

"Here you may rest tonight, my friend," Whirlwind said. "Tomorrow we will talk again."

The Cheyenne returned to his tipi and the men were soon fast asleep. The prairie was quiet in the early morning darkness. The sun would be up shortly, and the two former foes would continue their talk...

THE KIOWAS. Big Tree (Ado-Etta) (l) ca. 1890, and Satanta (Set-tain-te) (r), along with Satank, were arrested for the 1871 Warren Wagontrain Massacre in Texas; Satank was killed before the trial by soldiers whom he attacked; the other two were convicted by a Jacksboro jury and sentenced to hang. Texas Governor E.J. Davis commuted Big Tree and Satanta's sentences to life imprisonment, and they spent less than two years in Huntsville State Prison before being released in 1873 in a "deal" with the U.S. Army. A condition of their parole was that the Kiowas never again make war on the United States . For his part in the Red River War of 1874, however, Satanta was sent back to Huntsville - in chains as Whirlwind remembered - for the remainder of his life. Big Tree, although rearrested, was soon released. (Photos courtesy Frontier Originals, Topeka, Kansas, and Kansas State Historical Society, Topeka, Kansas).

Chapter 14

Farewell To The Chief
(May, 1876)

The sun was high when Wright awoke the next morning. Its warm rays creeping through the flap of his tipi and the bustle of those outside had awakened him. He dressed quickly and walked into the center of the Cheyenne camp. Children and dogs played everywhere and paid little attention to Wright as he wandered about their camp. Great chunks of buffalo meat were stretched across green poles balanced between two forked sticks as several women busily cooked over open fires. They turned the meat, occasionally pinching bites from it for themselves, and now and then, threw a piece to a large wolf-like dog sitting nearby.

After a typical Indian breakfast of buffalo meat, roasted corn, stewed pumpkin and various other vegetables, Wright sat down in the warm spring sun, dozing for awhile amidst the noise of children and dogs playing nearby. Chief Whirlwind was busy that morning and Wright did not disturb him to continue their talks of the previous evening. In the middle of the afternoon, a young brave ran into camp and everyone became very excited. When the commotion died down, Wright approached the chief.

"Is something wrong?" he asked.

"Nothing," Whirlwind replied sharply as he turned away and stood looking out across the prairie, his arms folded in anger.

Then he spoke. "Some crazy Comanches leave reservation. They look for scalps and ponies in Texas."

"There must be peace among all people," Wright cautioned. "Our fighting days are over. Remember, you said so last night."

"Me never fight again," Whirlwind said defiantly, still gazing at the prairie. Wright heard the sadness in his voice, and the old chief's expression conveyed his pain.

"War must stop. Me not fight. Indians and white man live together in peace," the chief emphasized once more, as if needing the assurance himself. His long gray hair glistened in the afternoon sun as Chief Whirlwind looked away; he did not speak again.

THE END OF AN ERA. Wright Mooar rode through the beautiful prairie land of Indian Territory and Kansas on his return to Dodge City. Just a few years later, "Boomers" set up camps like this one, poised, with the government's blessing, to take the land that had been set aside as Indian Territory. This picture was made at Arkansas City, Kansas on March 1, 1893. (Photo courtesy National Archives, Washington, D.C.)

74

The Cheyenne camp was restless for the next few days and Wright found little comfort in visiting any longer. John was already at Ft. Griffin and Wright planned to join him there. The Indians had blocked buffalo hunting in the Panhandle, and the hunters were determined to enter Texas from the East. Packing his gear, Wright made a brief stop at Chief Whirlwind's tipi.

The chief sat on the ground near the door, nodding a greeting as Mooar approached. Whirlwind stood.

Wright said, "We have lived together in peace for a few days. Can we not live together in peace always?"

The two friends clasped hands in farewell. "We live in peace," Whirlwind assured Mooar. "Me never fight white man again."

Indian children and dogs followed Wright as he rode out of the Cheyenne camp. Looking back over his shoulder he saw the chief standing in the center of the camp with his arms folded.

'Peace,' thought Wright Mooar. "The real peace is here on the prairie where buffalo once grazed.' Thoughts turning to Texas, he hurried his horse south. Wright made a brief stop at the Wichita Indian Agency where he spoke with Black Beaver, a Delaware chief.

"Chief Whirlwind has fled the reservation and gone north to help Sitting Bull," Black Beaver told Wright. It saddened Mooar that his friend had chosen to fight again.

Finishing his business with the Delawares, Mooar rode on. It would be a long, dangerous journey to Ft. Griffin, and Wright was anxious to be back in buffalo country again.

SCENES LIKE THIS were all too common to the Indians as buffalo hunting destroyed their way of life. The white hunter was so skilled at skinning out a buffalo he could do it in just minutes. Here, two skinners ply their trade. (Photo courtesy Scurry County Museum, Snyder, Texas)

Chapter 15

Texas, Vermont, Texas
(Summer & Fall, 1876)

Wright Mooar yearned for peace between the Indians and whites, but he also wanted to hunt buffalo again. He could see that the herds were dwindling as he rode across the prairies, and knew that buffalo hunting would soon be a thing of the past.

The trip to Texas was lonely and dangerous; Wright's only companion was a half-wolf dog he had gotten from some Arapahoes. At the slightest disturbance in the night, the dog pressed his paw against Wright's face.

"The dog was constantly alert and silent[9] during the night," Wright said later. "This was very unusual for this kind of dog."

In June, Mooar arrived at Ft. Griffin, an army outpost with its rough and rowdy satellite town, 150 miles west of Ft. Worth. The place was a haven for buffalo hunters, gamblers, ladies of ill repute, con artists, killers - and settlers traveling west. During Indian raids, local settlers sought shelter there.

Just as Wright arrived, John was preparing for a trip to Dallas with a load of hides; Wright decided to go along. Something happened to Wright on the trail; he became restless and impatient with the mule team's slow progress, and mounting his horse, rode ahead of John into Dallas. There, he boarded a train for New York where he visited their sister, then journeyed on to Vermont to the home of their parents.

His folks were eager to hear of their sons' adventures in the West, and they sat up late into the night listening to his stories. Wright visited old friends and seemed content to remain at Pownal for awhile. His father was ill and could not work, and Mooar was glad to help out around the old homeplace. Soon, though, typically J. Wright Mooar, he became restless.

When she learned he was leaving, Wright's mother urged him to find work in Pownal. He hated leaving with his father unable to work, but he wanted to return to the West. Within a few days, Wright packed and left for Philadelphia where he visited the great

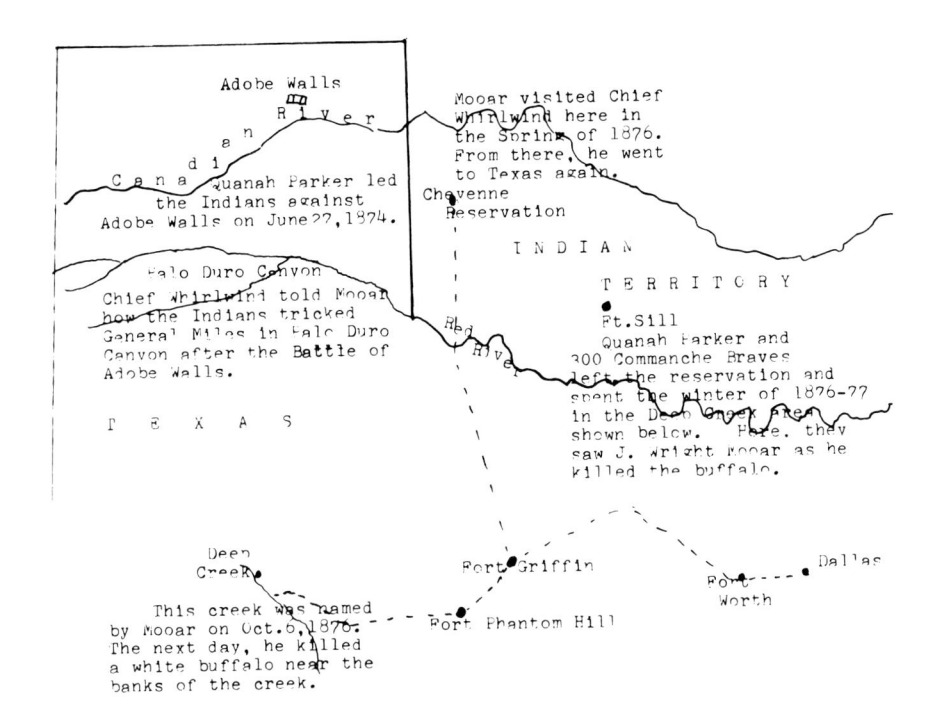

```
                    Adobe Walls
                         ☐☐
                       R i v e r
              a  n
           d  i
      C a n a  /Quanah Parker led      Mooar visited Chief
         the Indians against           Whirlwind here in
      Adobe Walls on June 27, 1874.    the Spring of 1876.
                                       From there, he went
         ┌─── Palo Duro Canyon         to Texas again.
         Chief Whirlwind told Mooar    Cheyenne
         how the Indians tricked       Reservation
         General Miles in Palo Duro
         Canyon after the Battle of              I N D I A N
         Adobe Walls.                                  T E R R I T O R Y
                                            Red       Ft. Sill
          T   E   X   A   S                    Riv    Quanah Parker and
                                                   \  300 Commanche Braves
                                                    \ left the reservation and
                                                      spent the winter of 1876-77
                                                      in the Deep Creek area
                                                      shown below.  Here, they
                                                      saw J. Wright Mooar as he
                                                      killed the buffalo.

                Deep                                                         Dallas
                Creek •                       Fort Griffin          •Fort•
             This creek was named                                    Worth
          by Mooar on Oct. 6, 1876.       Fort Phantom Hill
          The next day, he killed
          a white buffalo near the
          banks of the creek.
```

THE DOTTED LINES on this map show J. Wright Mooar's travels after he entered Texas in 1876; he left Dodge City, visited Whirlwind in Indian Territory, joined John at Ft. Griffin. Then, instead of hunting buffalo west of the fort as planned, Wright decided to visit his parents in Vermont. He returned to Ft. Griffin in late summer, then explored the Deep Creek area southwest of the fort, where he would build a home and live for over 65 years. (Map drawn by author).

Centennial Exposition. From there, he went to Ft. Worth, arriving in early September on one of the first trains into that town. J. Wright Mooar was ready to launch his last great hunt for buffalo in Texas.

He arrived at Ft. Griffin and found John camped about four miles from the fort. The wagons were already loaded with supplies for their move into an area west of Ft. Phantom Hill, about thirty miles away. The hunters were anxious to get started...

The long train, which had several teams of oxen, set out for the new hunting area. Because the mules were much faster than the oxen, the Mooars decided to divide the company into two groups. When they reached Ft. Phantom Hill, Wright took the mule teams and John came along behind with the oxen.

Reports had reached them that large herds of buffalo were in the divide between the Brazos and Colorado Rivers, and the outfits headed there to hunt. As Wright drove ahead, he left markers for John and his crew to follow. At the foot of a long hill, Wright came to the Clear Fork of the Brazos and stopped to replenish his water supply from a spring nearby. Pushing on west, he left the hills of the Clear Fork and set out across rolling open plains.

FT. GRIFFIN, TEXAS. An artist's concept of Ft. Griffin, c. 1876, about the time the Mooar company camped nearby on its way to Deep Creek in Scurry County, Texas. (Drawing courtesy Archives of the Southwest, Texas Tech University, Lubbock, Texas)

FT. PHANTOM HILL. Near Abilene, Texas, the ruins of Ft. Phantom Hill can still be seen today. In 1876, Wright and John Mooar stopped at this fort on their way to Scurry County to hunt buffalo in West Texas. (Photo courtesy Abilene Reporter News, Abilene, Texas)

This open country, dotted with low bushes and a sea of grass, reminded Wright of the Texas Panhandle region. There were signs everywhere that buffalo had passed through the area, but there were none in sight. The men pushed their teams farther west.

(About this same time, Charles Rath and his partner, Robert M. Wright left Dodge City headed for Texas to establish another supply station for the buffalo hunters and place to buy their hides. Wright Mooar, stated there were two to three hundred wagons that included John Russell, their head wagon master and his outfit, and sixty hunters. Rath headed his wagon train to an area northwest of what is now Abilene, and settled his outpost seventeen miles southeast of Double Mountains [a landmark for gold seekers on their way to California in 1849, as well as for General Marcy in his explorations of the Deep Creek area the same year].

The "town" was made up of buffalo hunters, settlers and other merchants, along with Rath's store, Charlie Sing's laundry house, a barber shop and "entertainment center" that included a saloon and brothel.

The firm of Lee and Reynolds, along with about forty women, soon joined the group at what was being called Rath City .

The outpost [sometimes called Camp Reynolds by editors] was short-lived; it faded and was gone by 1879 when the buffalo hunters left the area. It was, however, a place where Wright Mooar stopped occasionally when he hunted in that direction, or when he hauled his buffalo hides to Ft. Worth.

Rath City is noted locally for having been the town where Thomas (Tom) Lumpkins was shot and killed. Tom started a brawl in one of the town's saloons when he made a smart aleck remark about a recent Indian hunting venture by a group of his fellow hunters. He was killed by Limpy Jim Smith after having himself shot an unarmed hunter who was having his hair cut. Smith followed Lumpkins outside and shot him down in the street in front of George Aiken's saloon. Lumpkins was the first person to be buried in Rath City's boot hill cemetery... (Note: Hamlin, Texas hosts an annual celebration to commemorate the town of Rath City).

MOOAR CAMPSITE. Horses on the Hays Ranch graze on the 1876 campsite of Wright and his party of buffalo hunters on Deep Creek. Six hundred yards from this site, Mooar killed the white buffalo that would place his name in Texas and buffalo hunting history. (Photo by the author, Charles G. Anderson)

At the top of a large hill about thirty miles from the Clear Fork River, the Mooar party saw a low area dotted with trees; they knew there was a creek nearby. As they crossed the stream, Wright Mooar called it Deep Creek, so named because it cut so deeply into the prairie soil as it made its way toward the Colorado River.

That night, October 6, 1876, Mooar and his men camped on the south bank of Deep Creek. Early the next morning, they moved upstream toward the northwest hills. There, they hoped to find the great buffalo herd.

As he slept that night with his new Big Fifty Sharps rifle at his side, Wright Mooar did not realize that the land around this stream would become his home, nor that the next day, he would make Texas, and buffalo hunting, history...

THE CAPROCK. This escarpment has changed little over the last 120 years since Wright Mooar and his fellow hunters scouted the area looking for the last of the great buffalo herds. Pete Snyder hauled buffalo hides for the Mooar brothers in a wagon similar to this one. Pete moved with the hunters as they followed the herds, to be readily available when they needed a freighter to haul their hides to shipping points. But, he settled near Deep Creek, as did his friend and business associate, Wright Mooar. His "town," variously known as Hide Town and Robbers' Roost, was finally named Snyder in old Pete's honor. (Photo courtesy Scurry County Museum, Snyder, Texas)

Chapter 16

The White Buffalo
(October 7, 1876)

Arising at daybreak the next morning, Wright and his men moved out quickly toward the western hills. As they rode in the crisp autumn morning, they saw small bunches of buffalo, but the great herd was nowhere in sight. The men traveled hard along the creek for two hours. About ten o'clock, Wright pitched camp near the banks of Deep Creek. Hackberry, chinaberry and cottonwood trees grew thick and high along the creek banks, and the channel cut deeply into the rich soil as the water rushed downstream toward the Colorado.

Camp made, Wright mounted his horse and left to survey the country to the west.

ON THE MORNING OF OCTOBER 7, 1876, Mooar rode toward this Caprock to search for buffalo. Returning to Deep Creek late that evening, he killed the white buffalo. (Photo by the author, Charles G. Anderson)

"I'll be back about sundown," he told Dan Dowd, one of his hunters. Wright rode toward the hills and out onto the open plains. The countryside was ablaze with autumn colors. The sea of grass had turned purple and the October sun beamed down upon it all and blended it together in a dazzling array of color. From the edge of the plains, Wright looked down on the creek below. The trees along the stream were a rainbow, and the big cottonwood leaves fluttered in the fall breeze. Wright thought they looked very much like the maple trees of his home state of Vermont.

About two miles out on the plains, Wright reined his horse toward the southwest, where he saw beauty that few white men had ever seen. Small prairie lakes were brimming and rolling in white caps! This delighted his adventrous spirit. He saw sagebrush mingled with a sea of grass near the banks of a small creek; the land seemed to melt in the distance with the blue of the sky. Far to the west, the Caprock resembled the edge of a great bowl holding all the beauty of nature in this place for him.

Riding toward the Caprock, he traveled along the banks of the little creek, then turned back toward the east and headed toward Deep Creek. Wright had enjoyed the beauty of the plains, but was disappointed at not having located the buffalo herd. Anxious to reach camp, he galloped his horse for a time, and reached the hills west of camp just at sundown. The rays of the setting sun struck

J. WRIGHT MOOAR and Dan Dowd slipped up this creek bed to shoot the white buffalo. The cottonwood tree, under which the albino was standing, is no longer there. (Photo by the author, Charles G. Anderson)

glowing colors on the smoke from the campfires and provided a brilliant backdrop for the wagons.

Wright's vantage point gave him a panoramic view of the whole Deep Creek area. It looked like a giant stage with all western beauty laid out before him. As a boy in Vermont, Mooar had seen pictures of the West, but they had never compared with the real thing he was seeing now.

Suddenly, Wright spotted a small herd of buffalo on the eastern horizon not far from the wagons. The setting sun had flashed on a "white object in the midst of the herd."[10]

His heart raced rapidly as he decided on a course of action. Reining his horse quickly, Wright galloped down the hillside and into camp.

"How long has that herd been there?" he asked the men.

"They've been grazing this way for a couple of hours."

"Did you see the white buffalo!?" Mooar asked, excitedly.

The men said that they did not know a white buffalo was so near to hand; the news created a great deal of bustle in the camp. Only Dan Dowd accompanied Wright on the hunt; more might have caused the herd to stampede.

"Get your knife," Wright told Dowd. "We'll get some meat and a hide."

Dowd retrieved two knives from his pack, and the two men slipped out of camp and down into the banks of Deep Creek. They walked just along the water's edge to stay out of sight of the animals, traveling 600 yards in about twenty minutes. Every step was carefully chosen to avoid breaking a twig or kicking over a rock. Any extraordinary sound would send the buffalo herd stampeding toward the distant hills.

When they were in range of the buffalo, the two men peeked cautiously over the creek bank. The small herd, unaware of danger, grazed peacefully near a large cottonwood tree. The white buffalo stood out distinctly in the middle of the herd.

Wright and Dan slithered out of the creek and into the tall plains grass. The sun was almost down behind the western hills and dark shadows were slowly engulfing the creek bottom. The men knew they had to work fast before it was completely dark.

Mooar led the way through the grass toward the herd. The white buffalo, an albino freak of nature and a god to the native Indians, glistened in the last rays of the late evening sun.

The men gazed in awe at the unique creature standing before them. Wright raised his gun, but paused momentarily.

"Take a good look, Dan. There is the gamiest animal on earth, a white buffalo."[11]

Taking aim, Wright rested his elbow on the prairie grassland, leveled the sights on the albino standing under the cottonwood tree, and fired. The white buffalo fell in its tracks...

JUDY HAYS, J. Wright Mooar's granddaughter, sits atop the old fallen cottonwood tree under which her grandfather killed the white buffalo in October, 1876. (Photo courtesy Judy Hays, Snyder, Texas)

The rest of the herd milled in confusion, but as the hunters stood and walked toward the downed buffalo, the herd rushed toward them, led by a huge, snorting and bellowing black bull. Wright brought him to a thundering halt just a short distance from the hunters. He and Dowd killed two more bulls before the herd split and raced away. The whole affair had lasted only a few minutes, but Mooar and Dowd were drenched in sweat and totally exhausted.

The men marveled at the beauty of the white buffalo cow as she lay beneath the old cottonwood. Wright Mooar now understood why this beast was sacred and legendary to the Indians.

They quickly skinned the animal and hung the meat high in the tree, safe from coyotes and wolves that hunted in and around the creek bottoms at night. Wright Mooar was mighty proud when he and Dowd returned to camp that evening with the white buffalo hide. That day was the best of his adventures in the West.

JOHN WESLEY MOOAR (left) AND JOSIAH WRIGHT MOOAR (right), display the large hide of the albino buffalo cow that Wright killed near Deep Creek in western Texas on October 7, 1876. The hide is now in the possession of Judy Hays, Wright's granddaughter, who lives on the original Mooar Ranch near Snyder, Texas. (Photo courtesy Scurry County Museum, Snyder, Texas)

TWO VIEWS OF THE NOW DRY DEEP CREEK.. It was along the banks of this old stream that J. Wright Mooar and Dan Dowd crept up on the famous white buffalo. These photos were made in 1974, long after the stream had changed its course. (Photos by the author, Charles G. Anderson)

QUANAH PARKER was in the same area of west Texas where Wright Mooar hunted in 1876-1877. The Comanche chief led the attack against the buffalo hunters at Adobe Walls on the Canadian River in the Texas Panhandle in June, 1874. (Photo courtesy Kansas State Historical Society, Topeka, Kansas)

Chapter 17

Winter In Deep Creek Country
(1876-1877)

The next morning, Wright and two of the hunters retrieved the meat from the cottonwood tree. Others set out for the Clear Fork of the Brazos to look for John taking a hind quarter from the white buffalo with them. In the meantime, Wright explored north, west and east from his base camp, and as far to the south as the Colorado and Brazos Rivers. One night while lying awake near some of the other hunters, Wright overheard them talking quietly among themselves.

"Wonder how much farther that kid is going," one asked, " to try to find where the sun goes down?"[12]

Another replied, "Don't know, but I'd be ashamed not to follow when he volunteers to go ahead and find the way. Especially in these ravines that might be full of Indians."[13]

Wright never again hesitated to leave his outfit in the mens' hands while he was out scouting for buffalo.

The next day, he rode north; on the second morning, he was thirty miles from camp and still had not seen buffalo. About noon, however, he ran upon a big bull and fired from where he stood. The distance was 756 steps, the longest shot that Wright Mooar said he could ever remember making during his buffalo hunting days.

Unknown to the Mooars, Chief Quanah Parker and three hundred Comanche braves were in the same area of West Texas during the winter of 1876-1877.* They saw Wright kill the buffalo, and years later when asked about it, Parker said they did not attack Mooar because, "Your gun too big."

---

*Quanah Parker had been sent by government authorities at Ft. Sill to West Texas to talk the renegades into returning to their agency in Indian Territory. Parker chose a few hand-picked braves to accompany him to the Llano Estacado and Panhandle areas in his search for his fellow tribesmen.

When Wright returned to the Deep Creek camp, John had finally arrived with the oxen teams. He and the men had built dugout huts for their winter shelters, which were constructed by driving large cottonwood limbs into the ground, securing them at the top with strips of buffalo leather, and covering them with heavy layers of buffalo hides. A trench was then dug around the structure to carry away water.

Heavy snow and rain kept the Mooar outfit in camp for several days and gave them time for curing meat, scraping hides, cleaning rifles, and other 'housekeeping' chores necessary before another hunt could be undertaken.

Wright was determined to locate the great herd he knew in his heart still existed in Texas, snow and rain notwithstanding.

* * *

DURING THE WINTER, J. Wright Mooar and other hunters lived in dugouts similar to this one on the plains near Sheridan, Kansas.. (Photo courtesy the Kansas State Historical Society, Topeka, Kansas)

The winter of 1876-77 was extremely harsh in West Texas, but Mooar's success at hunting had brought other hunters into the Deep Creek area for the last of the buffalo in Texas. Small communities like the one located at Rath City (Camp Reynolds) near Double Mountain (northeast of Scurry County) attracted a great number of hunters. (One of them was Pat Garrett, later sheriff of Lincoln County, New Mexico, who would become famous as the man who shot and killed Billy the Kid). These buffalo hunting camps were located for fifty miles or more around Deep Creek.

The area at the foot of Double Mountain on what is now Sweetwater Creek in northern Scurry County, was much used by Mooar and his contemporaries; hunters could usually find a few buffalo grazing along the Double Mountain Fork where they came for water. One of Mooar's hunter friends, James (Jim) Ennis, had an unusual experience that winter while he was camped in the area.

Ennis was hunting alone on foot in a heavy morning ground fog; he had killed several bulls and had wounded another. Following the buffalo trying for a better shot, he got too close to the wounded animal in the heavy fog. Hurt and frightened, the bull whirled on the hunter and charged him. Ennis dropped his gun and ran for a dead mesquite tree that stood nearby. The buffalo hit the tree head-on and it snapped off dropping the hunter onto the animal's back. Jim rolled off, but a forked limb from the dead tree landed on the bull's back and the frightened animal ran away.

Alone and lost, Ennis finally stumbled across one of his skinned out buffaloes, and it now being near dusk, he decided to make camp there for the night. He cooked and ate some of the buff meat, then spread the hide, hair up, on the ground and rolled himself up in it to sleep.

During the night, a "blue norther" (storms famous in West Texas for their suddenness) blew into the area and in the extreme cold, the buffalo hide froze, encasing Jim Ennis. Attracted by the freshly killed meat, a pack of lobo wolves began feeding on the buffalo carcass nearby, and finally began eating away the flesh Ennis had left on the skinned-out hide in which he was now encased.

Despite his yelling and screaming, the wolves continued their feast, sometimes tearing Ennis' clothing as they chewed through the buffalo hide. The lobos fed throughout the night and finally left with the dawn. By mid-morning, the sun had thawed the buffalo hide enough that Jim could unroll himself.

About noon, the skinners in Ennis' camp saw an old, bent and wrinkled, white haired man walking toward them carrying Jim's gun and wearing his clothes. Alarmed that someone had killed their boss, the men were extreme in their questioning of the man. After hearing his story, they finally realized that this apparition was their friend and boss, Jim Ennis, who had left camp just the day before a black haired and upright man in his prime. His experiences with the wounded buffalo and lobo wolves had left him an old man they did not recognize![14]

Wright Mooar first told this story to a young historian, J. Evetts Haley, in a letter written to him on November 27, 1927. Mooar often entertained young people like Earl McDow, Brud Boren, Roy Hendrix and others at his ranch on cold winter nights by telling this story of his friend, Jim Ennis. The young folks huddled on buffalo robes, sometimes even the famous white hide, in front of a fireplace listening to Wright Mooar's stories.

Jim Ennis, like Mooar, was one of the last hunters to see the great herds of buffalo in Scurry County, Texas. Both of these old hunters were later honored by the citizens of the county by having landmarks named for them; (Ennis Creek, noted by Wright Mooar in his 1933 *Holland's Magazine* article; and the Mooar School).

Within two years, the buffalo were gone from Texas, and Mooar and Ennis would never again hunt the big shaggies. With the demise of the buffalo, the Indians as well as the hunters were also gone. An era had passed and would only be relived in stories like those told by J. Wright Mooar about those colorful days of high adventure and danger, of friends like Jim Ennis, and of enemies now gone, never to return.

A BUFFALO HUNTERS' SUMMER CAMP, C. 1878. Buffalo were skinned and the hides scraped of the flesh still attached to the underside. Then they were stretched on poles or were staked to the ground, When the hides dried, they were stacked in mule or oxen drawn wagons and freighted to Dodge City, Kansas or Ft. Worth, Texas. These photos also show buffalo meat hanging to cure for the hunters' ready supply of food, or for sale in the towns. (Photos courtesy Scurry County Museum, Snyder, Texas)

MANY INDIANS ESCAPED their reservations and banded together for raids against the encroaching whites. The U.S. Government began sending the 'renegades' far away from their hereditary homes. Here, in a photo dated September 10, 1886, a band of Mescalero Apaches on their way to Florida, are shown at a rest stop beside a Southern Pacific Railway near Neuces River, Texas. In the center front is Natchez, and to his left are Geronimo and his son who wear matching shirts. (Photo courtesy National Archives, Washington, D.C. Photo by A.J. McDonald)

Chapter 18

Other Ventures
(1877-1878)

Buffalo on the American plains were disappearing at an alarming rate. Hunters by the hundreds gave up their short, but adverturous occupation, many moving farther west to mine for gold, copper or silver, or to work for the quickly developing Santa Fe Railroad Company. The Mooar brothers realized that they, too, would have to branch out into other business endeavors if they were to remain in the West.

In the summer of 1877, they bought five hundred head of cattle from John Goff who had a spread near Double Mountain on the Clear Fork of the Brazos. They built a house for their ranching headquarters at the mouth of Cottonwood Creek and began cattle ranching in earnest. Just as with buffalo hunting, the Mooars determined to make a success of the new venture.

DEEP CREEK, C. 1910. J. Wright Mooar, Pete Snyder and others settled near Deep Creek in the late 1870s. Many lived in dugouts along its banks, as they hunted buffalo in the area. (Photo courtesy Georgene Galloway, Snyder, Texas)

Wright tried desperately to maintain an interest in the cattle and trading businesses, but the mundane chores of the ranch bored him and he soon became restless. Eventually, he was spending more and more time at the old Deep Creek campsite searching for buffalo. Mooar could not give up the dream of once more locating the great Texas herd he had seen at the Arkansas River years ago...

Other hunters who had turned to ranching on the side, moved in and around Deep Creek and Wright felt their intrusion upon the land he had discovered and which he had learned to love. As they explored the area and killed the last remaining buffaloes, the hunters named the creeks and streams they came across. As Wright continued his search for the great herd, he crossed Bull Creek, so named by Charley Hart because he had killed many buffalo bulls near its banks. Other men, Moore, Gavitte and Jim Ennis, placed their names on the streams where they hunted as well.

PETE AND NELLIE SNYDER are shown shortly after their wedding. Snyder left Hide Town (Snyder) for Colorado (City), Texas in 1881. He is buried there in the city cemetery. (Photo courtesy Colorado City Museum, Colorado City, Texas)

THE MOOAR RANCH. As the buffalo disappeared, the Mooar's began cattle ranching. Here, cowboys herd cattle into pens at the ranch. (Photo courtesy Judy Hays)

Thoughout the winter of 1877-78, Wright hunted the Deep Creek region, but someone else had always been there before him; buffalo were practically non-existent in the area.

And, to make matters worse, his old freighting friend, Pete Snyder had opened a trading post just ten miles from Wright's Deep Creek campsite. Hunters and cattlemen made the new outpost their trading headquarters. The place was being called Hide Town. (Later, it would be known variously as Robber's Roost and Snyder's Place.)

Wright saw a rapid end to his buffalo hunting and was frantic to find the big herd he knew must be somewhere west of Deep Creek. He rode to the ranch to talk with John.

"I'm sorry to leave, but I've got to find that buffalo herd! Will you take care of the ranch for awhile?"

Assured that his brother would care for their businesses while he was away, Wright Mooar rode back to Deep Creek, then headed west toward the high plains.

JUDY HAYS. Wright Mooar's granddaughter, Judy Hays, sits near the old well her grandfather dug on the banks of Deep Creek when he lived there in a dugout. Mooar later built a beautiful home near this site. (Photo courtesy Judy Hays, Snyder, Texas)

Chapter 19

Wright Finds The Last Great Buffalo Herd
(Spring, 1878)

The snow had melted and the days were springlike as Wright and his men rode toward the Caprock. They'd had some fairly good buffalo hunting, but they needed more hides to supply their market. Small herds began coming out of the canyons to graze on the greening grass of the open plains.

By early May, Mooar's crew had killed over three thousand buffalo. These hides and 25,000 pounds of meat were taken back to the Deep Creek campsite to be dried and processed. Pete Snyder then hauled the hides and meat to Ft. Worth where the hides were shipped by train back East, and the meat sold locally.

The meat was cut into hams then divided into four large sections, salted and packed in brine. After several days, the meat was hung in a smoke house for final processisng.

The smoke house was a hackberry pole structure covered with stretched buffalo hides which were nailed to the poles with eight penny nails brought from Ft. Worth by Pete Snyder. These smoke houses were over a hundred feet long and about twenty feet wide. Pits were dug in the ground and hackberry and chinaberry logs were burned under the meat for ten to twelve days.

The smoked buffalo meat would keep unspoiled for many weeks, and was quite tasty. A hunter once remarked that smoked buff meat was "thoroughly medicated."

Although the Mooar party had been successful with their hunting, Wright was not satisfied; he still had not located the great herd. He slipped out of camp once more and rode about seventy miles northwest, hoping to find them in the canyons there.

One morning he sighted a cow coming toward him over a small hill. Wright raised his Sharps rifle and dropped the buffalo with one shot. "Pandemonium broke loose," he recalled later. "I thought the world had come to an end!"

The cow was an advance for some 20,000 buffalo hidden from sight in the far side of the hill! At his shot, they instantly broke into a stampede, many of them heading directly for his stand. When Mooar heard the hooves pounding the hard ground, he was already standing near the fallen cow. Trapped with no place to go, he crouched behind the dead buffalo as the leaders split the herd and thundered by.

Back at camp, he told the men of the thirteen buffalo that had been trampled to death by the stampede, their mangled bodies lying near his hiding place behind the cow. Wright had bruises of his own, as he hobbled back into the Deep Creek camp.

This was J. Wright Mooar's narrowest escape from death in all his days of buffalo hunting. He did not know it then, but he had just seen the last of the great buffalo herds in West Texas. Hunting in this region would cease before another winter passed.

TYPICAL WEST TEXAS hillside. Mooar watched as a lone cow topped a hill; he shot her and was in the process of skinning the animal when the main herd stampeded right at him. The cow had been the advance scout for the last of the great Texas buffalo herds of over 20,000 animals. (Photo by the author, Charles G. Anderson)

Chapter 20

Westward To Arizona
(April, 1879 - November, 1880)

The last scattered West Texas buffalo herds fell to Wright Mooar's gun in March, 1879. Unable - or unwilling - to settled down to ranch life or trading, he decided to try another business venture in Arizona Territory.

In April, 1879, he set out for Prescott and Phoenix with two mule drawn wagons and a seventeen-year-old boy as his only companion. John, and Wright's friends from the Deep Creek area, tried to no avail to dissuade him going on such a dangerous trek without more protection. The Apache Geronimo had vowed vengeance on all whites in New Mexico and Arizona, and Victorio, head of a guerilla band of Mescaleros and Chiricahuas, was also raiding into those territories from his hideout in the mountains of northern Mexico. It didn't matter; Wright was going...

He and the boy traveled west and the days grew longer and hotter. Rather than Indians, the desert sun and wind were the forces that almost drove them back to Texas. Water was scarce, and the inexperienced youngster proved an additional hardship on Wright. In spite of the difficulties, however, after fifty-six days of hard travel - and no encounters with Indians! - they reached Prescott, the territorial capital of Arizona.

The business climate here was good. Prescott had become the capital just two years earlier and things were booming. Wright sold the dried buffalo meat immediately for twenty cents a pound, and moved south to the little village of Phoenix.

In 1877, the Southern Pacific Railroad Company was bringing the railroad across America. Suddenly, the federal government had refused permission for further construction in Arizona Territory, and all railroad building was halted at Phoenix. By the time Mooar arrived there, however, the Southern Pacific had received permission to resume construction. Almost immediately, Wright began hauling freight for the company, as well as for the important mining industry around Prescott and Phoenix.

MULE DRAWN FREIGHT WAGONS. Wright Mooar used wagons like these for his freighting business in Arizona in 1879-1880. (Photo courtesy Cy Martin Collection, from The Saga of the Buffalo, Hart Publications, 1973)

    He tried hard to be a good businessman, and for awhile, Wright did well. He invested some of the money from the buffalo meat sales in additional teams of mules and wagons, and he had several men working for him. As he freighted materials from one place to another for the railroad, he sometimes bought and sold goods and supplies on the side. The miners always needed flour, and Wright often took a full load to them.

    On all his trips, Mooar carried his buffalo gun, which had not been fired in about two years. One morning in September, 1880, as Wright looked out across the cactus-dotted Sonoran desert toward Texas, he thought of Deep Creek with its cottonwoods, chinaberrys and hackberrys. His thoughts of the peaceful Texas countryside drew him like a magnet.

    In that minute, Mooar decided to return to Deep Creek, and asked the young man who had accompanied him west if he wanted to go back with him; the boy chose to stay in Arizona.

    By the end of that day, Wright had sold his freighting outfit, but kept his best team of mules. He hitched them to a hack, and the next day headed for Ft. Griffin, Texas.

Traveling alone was long and hard; he slept little because of warnings of Indian raids he received at the string of military forts along his way. Shortly after leaving El Paso, he heard that Victorio and his whole band of warriors had been killed nearby on October 14. Wright had traveled through the area just a few days before...

At night, he slept at least three hundred yards away from his hack, his rifle always at his side. Awake at the slightest sound, Wright immediately cradled the gun. He sometimes saw Indians in the distance, but none of them attacked.

On the evening of November 5, 1880, Mooar pulled into Ft. Griffin. He had been on the trail for thirty days and was tired and weary, but very happy to be back in Texas. After a short visit with the commander at Ft. Griffin, he purchased necessary supplies, and headed west toward Deep Creek... home.

Pete Snyder's little trading post had grown into a small community and Wright saw changes all over the countryside. Ranches had been staked off, and where buffalo roamed just two years earlier, cattle now grazed on the lush grass. The Nunn brothers were grazing cattle along Deep Creek and Mooar felt uneasy in his old campsite near the stream. Nevertheless, he was glad to be back...

GRADING RAILROAD BEDS NEAR COLORADO (CITY), TEXAS. Teams of mules were used to build railroads in the 1880-90s. The Texas Pacific Railroad Company hired the Mooar brothers to supply hay for their animals. (Photo courtesy Colorado City Museum, Colorado City, Texas)

Epilogue

(1880-1940)

J. Wright Mooar's story did not end with his return to Deep Creek, although his buffalo hunting days were over. The remaining strays had disappeared while he was in Arizona.

John had worked hard in their Texas enterprises and was then supplying hay for the animals of the Texas and Pacific Railroad Company, which was grading rights of way near Colorado (City). The Mooars were kept busy in this venture until the railroad reached Pecos, Texas.

In 1880, the town of Colorado (City) was established and Wright and John opened a livery stable there. The town was bustling with the growing cattle business in the area, and the Mooars were very successful.

In 1881, Pete Snyder moved to Colorado (City) from Hide Town, but the community that sprang up around his trading post continued to grow. Many locals still called the town "Snyder's Place," but it was not until July 2, 1907 that its name became Snyder.

The Mooars maintained their ranching near the Clear Fork of the Brazos, but soon needed more land for their growing herd of cattle. They purchased a large tract west of Snyder on Deep Creek in 1883, and by 1884, the brothers had 1,500 head of cattle, 30 saddle horses and 100 stock horses. This ranch became a part of

J. W. MOOAR BROS.,

AGENTS FOR HYNES BUGGY CO.

SALES YARDS FOR NORTHERN CATTLE.

LIVERY AND FEED STABLE.

LETTERHEAD from the Mooar brothers' livery stable business, begun in 1880 in Colorado (City), Texas. (Courtesy Scurry County Museum, Snyder, Texas)

MOOAR LIVERY STABLES. A.R. Wood (left) and an unidentified co-worker at the Mooar brothers stables in Colorado (City), Texas. This business was established by the partnership in 1881. (Photo courtesy Colorado City Museum, Colorado City, Texas)

Scurry County, which was formed by an act of the Texas Legislature in 1876.* Wright and John continued their partnership for a few more years, but eventually split the business going their separate ways.

On April 13, 1897, Wright married Mrs, Julia Swartz at Colorado (City). He continued ranching in the Deep Creek area and built a large home there in 1908. Wright spent most of his remaining years near Deep Creek; the plains and rolling hills nestled against the western Caprock gave him peace and comfort. Mooar was proud of the accomplishments of his early western years, and he spoke to civic groups about his adventures. He took great pride in showing off the white buffalo hide, and often told the story of having been offered $5,000 for the robe by President Theodore Roosevelt, whom he had met in 1904 in St. Louis, Missouri.

---

* The Texas Legislature honored the memory of Confederate General William Read Scurry when they named a vast area of West Texas for him on August 21, 1876. The county, however, was not officially organized until governing officials were elected by the populace on June 28, 1884.

J. Wright Mooar died in 1940 and was laid to rest in the Snyder Cemetery near the grave of his late wife, Julia, who had died in 1921. People came from all over Scurry County, and from throughout the state to honor the memory of the old buffalo hunter. His funeral was conducted, at his wish, in the First Methodist Church of Snyder by Wright's Masonic Lodge; he had been a Mason for over 50 years. Mooar had known Snyder, Texas as Robber's Roost and Hide Town, names unfamiliar to most people in town in 1940, but Mooar remembered them well...

* * *

MR. & MRS. J. WRIGHT MOOAR. Julia and Wright pictured in their later years. The two had married in 1897 and their interest in West Texas made them leading citizens both in Snyder and Colorado (City), Texas. The couple lived in a grand house built near Deep Creek by Wright in 1908. Julia died in 1921, Wright in 1940. (Photo courtesy Colorado City Museum, Colorado City, Texas)

JULIA SWARTZ MOOAR. She met Wright Mooar at Colorado (City), Texas, and married him in 1897. (Photo courtesy Colorado City Museum, Colorado City, Texas)

J. WRIGHT MOOAR. He was 46 years old when he met and married Mrs. Julia Swartz. Photo was made a few years after their marriage. (Photo from Judy Hays)

J. WRIGHT AND JULIA MOOAR. The sitting couple is believed to be Wright's parents, John Allen and Esther K. Mooar. The elder Mooars visited Wright and Julia at Deep Creek for a short time, but returned to their home in Vermont. (Photo Courtesy Judy Hays.)

108

BUILDING A TOWN. When buffalo hunting ceased, former buffalo hunters and other settlers began building towns. This 1904 view of Snyder, Texas, formerly Hide Town or Robber's Roost, shows the center of the community with its pubic well where all the inhabitants came for water. (Photo courtesy Scurry County Museum, Snyder, Texas)

PICNIC DAY IN SNYDER, 1912. This yellow brick courthouse was completed in 1911. The photo shows a group of Snyder residents gathered for a picnic. (Photo courtesy Scurry Museum, Snyder, Texas)

Pete Snyder's Map of Snyder, Texas

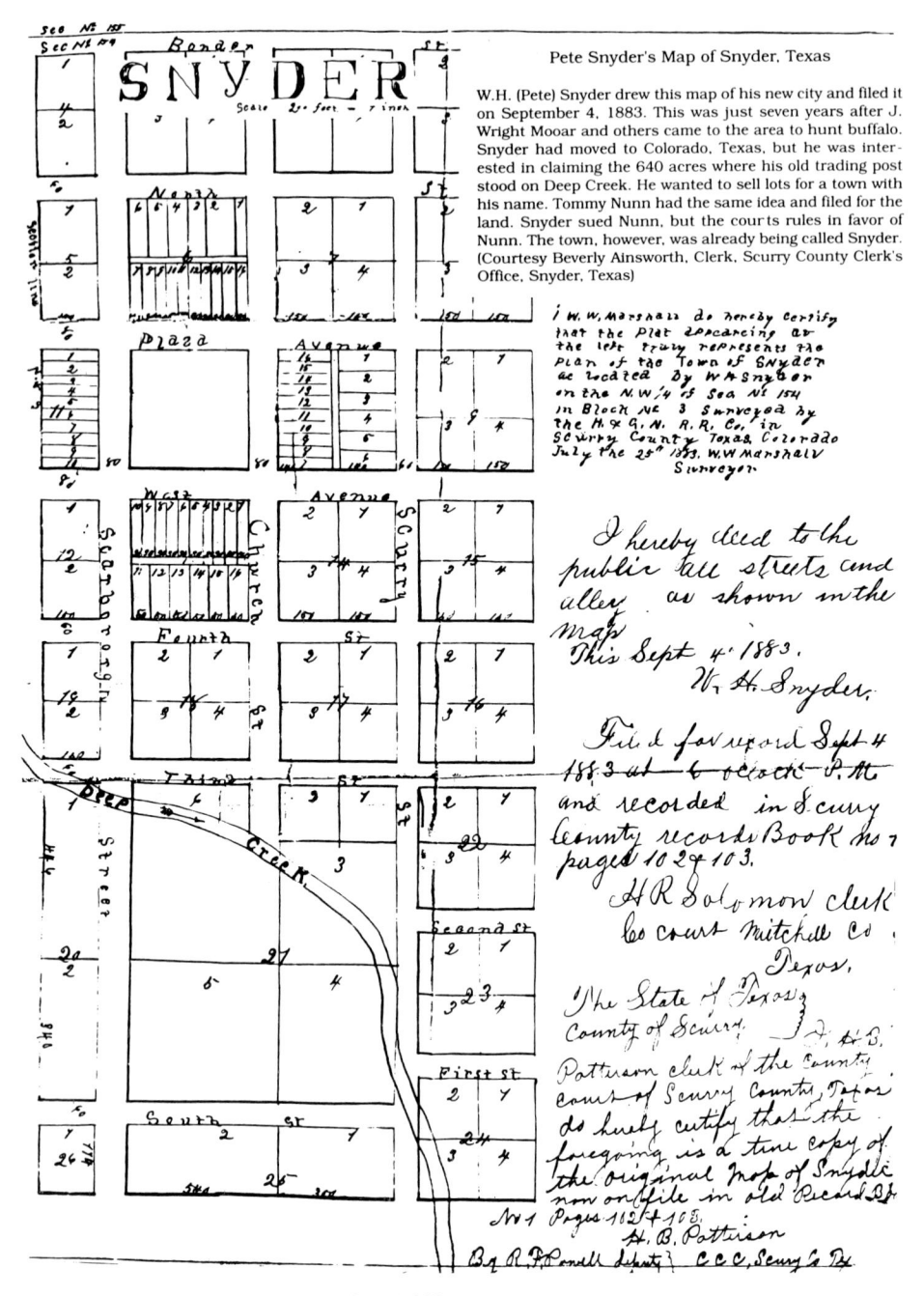

W.H. (Pete) Snyder drew this map of his new city and filed it on September 4, 1883. This was just seven years after J. Wright Mooar and others came to the area to hunt buffalo. Snyder had moved to Colorado, Texas, but he was interested in claiming the 640 acres where his old trading post stood on Deep Creek. He wanted to sell lots for a town with his name. Tommy Nunn had the same idea and filed for the land. Snyder sued Nunn, but the courts rules in favor of Nunn. The town, however, was already being called Snyder. (Courtesy Beverly Ainsworth, Clerk, Scurry County Clerk's Office, Snyder, Texas)

PLAT MAP OF SNYDER, TEXAS, c. 1883.

COLORADO (CITY), MITCHELL COUNTY, TEXAS, C. 1883. This artist's rendering, drawn by Augustus Koch, shows Colorado City, platted in July, 1881, as it appeared two years later. The Colorado River runs through town, the main section connected to outlying residences by the bridge on Concho Street and what may be a foot bridge near the railroad trestle. In 1881, there were 12 merchants, 5 saloons, 2 livery stables, 2 wagon yards, 2 lawyers, 3 hotels and 1 restaurant. By the time this drawing was made, a courthouse, county jail, railroad depot and an opera house had been built. (Photo courtesy Colorado City Museum, Colorado City, Texas)

Standing near Wright Mooar's grave, one can see the trees that still surround Deep Creek as it winds its way through the town of Snyder. But the buffalo, like the hunters and bands of nomadic Indians who hunted them, have all disappeared from the region. Mooar never apologized for the twenty odd thousand of the big shaggies that he killed, maintaining until he died that it was necessary for the civilization of the American West.

Historians will always argue about the slaughter of close to four million buffalo during the 1870s, but to Wright Mooar and the other hunters, it was a business, an adventure. The fact that history was made in the process did not necessarily drive the men, but they knew they were a part of an era that was passing, and would never again happen in America.

Now, one might look around this area of West Texas and feel a little of the excitement that Wright experienced in October, 1876 when he stopped at the top of a hill just east of Deep Creek. Here, he decided, as he gazed over the new countryside, he would make his home.

J. WRIGHT MOOAR'S HOUSE, c. 1910. On the site where Wright killed the white buffalo, he planted pecan trees, dug a well and built this house in 1908. The people in the picture are unidentified. (Photo courtesy Scurry County Museum, Snyder, Texas)

MOOAR HOME. J. Wright Mooar (second from left) is shown with friends at his home, c. 1929. Francene Allen-Noah, former teacher in the Snyder ISD, gave the following information about the photo: "B. F. Womack, Sr., my grandfather, is on the far left, J. Wright Mooar, Wayne Boren, 'Booger Red' Townsend, Mrs. Womack, Tommy McDonnell and Mamie Booth McDonnell." (Photo courtesy Scurry County Museum, Snyder, Texas; identification, Francene Allen-Noah)

THE MOOAR HOME, c. 1974. In later years, this elegant structure, built ten miles northwest of Snyder, fell into decay and was finally taken down in the 1970s. (Photo by the author, Charles G. Anderson)

Today in Snyder one can find many reminders of its bygone years. The Historical Commission maintains a large collection on J. Wright Mooar in the museum of Western Texas College, built in 1971 near the banks of Deep Creek.

Large ranches, including Wright Mooar's (now owned by his granddaughter, Mrs. S.D. (Judy) McDonnell Hays, Jr.) are still located around Snyder, Texas. Herds of fine cattle and horses now graze where buffalo once roamed. The whole area became one of the richest oil producing regions in America in the mid-20th century. Many of the old ranchers who weathered the depression of the 1930s and managed to hang onto their land, became wealthy when the oil industry boomed in 1950.

And, on the square of the Scurry County Courthouse in Snyder, Texas, stands a giant statue of a white buffalo, placed there by grateful citizens of the town to honor a 19th century Vermont adventurer who traveled half-way across the continent in search of the buffalo, and ended his days in West Texas as an American legend...

Appendix I

J. Wright Mooar's Guns

THE BIG FIFTYS. Judy Hays, granddaughter of J. Wright Mooar, stands in front of the 120-year old white buffalo, killed by her famous grandfather in October, 1876. Judy holds both Wright's "Big Fifty" Sharps rifles: The white buffalo fetish necklace was carved by the grandson of Comanche Chief Quanah Parker, Monroe Tomahakara. (Photo by the author, Charles G. Anderson).

MOOAR'S SHARPS RIFLES. **Top**: The .50-90 Model 1874 Sharps Mooar owned in 1874, lighter 30", octagon to round barrel, double set triggers, a Hartford style forearm, and open barrel sights, serial number C54246. The list price for this rifle was $42.00; it was originally shipped August 3, 1874 to Dodge City, Kansas Sharps dealer, F.C. Zimmerman, located on Front Street. It is fairly certain that Wright purchased the Sharps while he was in Dodge and brought it with him to Texas. The Mooar family sold the rifle to Ben Weathers, who sold it to Will Berry, from whom the Heritage Museum in Fredericksburg, Texas purchased it. The Scurry County Museum now owns the Mooar Sharps.

Bottom: It is believed that J. Wright Mooar bought this .50-90 Sharps Rifle in New York in 1876 while visiting his sister on a whirlwind trip to see his family. It was originally invoiced to J.P. Moore & Sons of New York City on September 5, 1876. On his return to Texas that fall, Mooar entered the area that is now Scurry County and killed the white buffalo possibly with this rifle on October 7, 1876. This Sharps is a bigger gun than the one above. It also has an octogon to round barrel, but it is shorter and much heavier, hence the name Big Fifty. It also has open barrel sights and double set triggers; serial number 156645. The Mooar family sold this rifle to Ben Weathers, who in turn sold it to "Mule" Kayser and Bill Emerson. The Hays' (Mooar's granddaughter, Judy and her husband S.D.), brought it back into the family to the tune of $1,500. The gun now resides in their home along with the white buffalo robe. An interesting characteristic of both Sharps is the wear on the right sides of the forearms. Both seem to have been either worn or broken off down to the bottom edge of the side flat of the octagon section. (Photo by the author Charles G. Anderson).

MR. & MRS. S.D. HAYS. *Judy and S.D. hold the 1874 Sharps 50-90s that once belonged to her grandfather; she has the Big Fifty, which she and S.D. now own, and he holds the lighter Hartford model. Behind them is the famous white buffalo robe, which is permanently displayed in their home on the original J. Wright Mooar ranch near Snyder, Texas. (Photo by the author Charles G. Anderson).*

ARTIFACTS. *Displayed alongside the white buffalo robe and other memorabilia that once belonged to J. Wright Mooar, are a .50 bullet mould, a bullet cast from the mould, a finished .50-90 cartridge, and a chunk of lead recently located at the old Mooar campsite on Deep Creek. (Photo by the author Charles G. Anderson).*

MOOAR'S HENRY. Close-up of a Henry lever action rifle once owned by J. Wright Mooar. It is .44-40, has a 24" barrel and is serial numbered 3611. Wright gave this rifle to Dr. H.G. Towle who at his death, left the Henry to his son-in-law, Dr. John Blum. The rifle now belongs to Dr. Robert Pierce, who obtained it from Blum. (Dr. Pierce stated that Wright Mooar found a Sharps' rifle on the battlefield where Ranald S. Mackenzie fought the Comanches on Sweetwater Creek. This Sharps is allegedly owned by an individual in Uvalde, Texas. (Photo by the author Charles G. Anderson).

HENRY RIFLE. One of four guns owned by J. Wright Mooar, this .44-40 Henry rifle is now the property of Dr. Robert Pierce of Snyder, Texas. (Photo by the author Charles G. Anderson).

JUDY HAYS. Granddaughter of J. Wright Mooar stands before the white buffalo robe with Mooar's Big Fifty Sharps Rifle. The hide is permanently displayed at Mrs. Hays' home in Scurry County, Texas. (Photo courtesy Snyder Daily News, Noble Young, photographer - ca. 1983).

Appendix II

A West Texas Photo Album
(1876-1994)

J. WRIGHT MOOAR, c. 1910. In his later years, Wright sat for long hours extoling his exploits among the buffalo and the Indians to youngsters. (Photo courtesy Scurry County Museum, Snyder, Texas)

J. WRIGHT MOOAR. Aboard his horse, and holding the Big Fifty Sharps Rifle from his buffalo hunting days, Mooar is ready as Grand Marshal, to lead Snyder's 1936 Texas Centennial Parade. (Photo courtesy Elaine Rosser Lambert, Snyder, Texas)

J. WRIGHT MOOAR AND FRIENDS, c. 1929. (Left to right) Dr. H.G. Towle, A.C. Wilmeth, J. Wright Mooar, O.P. Thrane, Jody Monroe and Tom McDonnell (Mooar's adopted son). (Photo courtesy Archives of the Southwest, Texas Tech University, Lubbock, Texas)

SCURRY COUNTY'S FIRST COURTHOUSE, c. 1891. Scurry County was just two years old when this courthouse was completed in 1886. Posing here in 1891 are (left to right) Jim Nunn, Old Man Grant, (Unknown), Houston Patterson, Grandpa Byrd, Frank Wylks, Ira Kutch, Walter Grantham, (Unknown), William Bell, Az Wood and Oz Smith. (Photo courtesy Scurry County Museum, Snyder, Texas)

OLD ENGINE NO. 1, c. 1907. This engine was the first purchased by the Roscoe, Snyder and Pacific Railway. J.W. Green is the man in the black suit near the engine. (Photo courtesy Scurry County Museum, Snyder, Texas)

JOHN W. MOOAR, JR. Son of Wright's brother, John Wesley. His father was credited with opening the buffalo hide trade in the East when Wright sent 50 hides to him in New York which were purchased by Pennsylvania tanners. (Photo courtesy Colorado City Museum, Colorado City, Texas)

LYDIA LOUISE "DOT" MOOAR. John Wesley's daughter. Miss Mooar thought her father had been overlooked in buffalo hunting and Texas history, because of the fame his brother had gained in killing the white buffalo. (Photo courtesy Colorado City Museum, Colorado City, Texas)

PETE SNYDER'S RANCH. Snyder worked with the Mooar brothers for many years and settled near them in Colorado (City), Texas in 1881. Later, he bought a ranch near a small community located between Snyder and Colorado City. The settlement was often called Hell Roarin' Holler. (Photo courtesy Scurry County Museum, Snyder, Texas)

OLDTIMERS AT PETE SNYDER'S RANCH, c. 1984. Dewey Denson (center), says this was Pete and Nellie Snyder's ranch, the original windmill in the background. Most of these men knew Snyder and Wright Mooar. (Left to right) Hack Billingsley, Martin Murphy, Denson, Arlie Taylor, Fred Cotton. (Photo by the author Charles G. Anderson)

MOOAR BURIAL SITES. J. Wright and Julia Swartz Mooar are buried in the old Snyder, Texas cemetery in a simple plot near his adopted son, Tom McDonnell and family. Judy Hays is the daughter of McDonnell, and the Mooar's granddaughter. (Photos by the author Charles G Anderson).

THE MCDONNELLS. Thomas J. McDonnell was the adopted son of J. Wright and Julia Mooar, to whom they left their estate. The elder Mooars are buried beside Mamie K. and Thomas J. in this plot in the Snyder city cemetery. (Photo by the author Charles G. Anderson)

COLORADO CITY, TEXAS CEMETERY. Pete and Nellie Snyder are buried here in the Snyder plot in Colorado City, Texas. (Photo courtesy Colorado City Museum, Colorado City, Texas)

WRIGHT MOOAR AND GRANDDAUGHTER, JUDY HAYS. At the 1936 Texas Centennial Parade in Snyder. Mooar was the Grand Marshal for the parade. (Photo courtesy Elaine Rosser Lambert, Snyder, Texas)

JUDY HAYS joins descendants of Quanah Parker in the annual White Buffalo Celebration in Snyder, Texas, October, 1994. (Photo by the author Charles G. Anderson)

MONROE TOMAHAKARA, grandson of Quanah Parker rides in the White Buffalo Celebration Parade in 1994. (Photo by the author Charles G. Anderson)

WHITE BUFFALO DAYS,, SNYDER, TEXAS, OCTOBER 7, 1995. The author, Charles Anderson, (left) and Hugh "Brud" Boren (right). Boren, more than any other Scurry County individual has helped preserve the history of the white buffalo. When "Brud" was a young man, he spent many hours at the Mooar home listening to Wright's stories of the Old West. (Photo by the author Charles G. Anderson)

ELMER KELTON. Award winning writer, Elmer Kelton (left) and author Charles Anderson (right) attend the 1995 White Buffalo Days Celebration in Snyder, Texas. (Photo by the author Charles G. Anderson)

THE WHITE BUFFALO. This statue was erected in 1967 by the citizens of Scurry County. School children donated pennies to help purchase the monument as a memorial to J. Wright Mooar. (Photo by the author Charles G. Anderson)

UNVEILING THE WHITE BUFFALO, 1994. Artist Robert Taylor (left) stands with Judy Hays, Wright Mooar's granddaughter (center back) and Comanche Chief Monroe Tomahakara, grandson of Quanah Parker. Mooar and Parker became friends later in their lives. (Students unidentified). (Photo by the author Charles G. Anderson)

The Legend of the White Buffalo

J. Wright Mooar came to seek his fortune
In a land not widely known.
He left his mark for all to see
In a legend, not a stone.

He made his camp at Deep Creek
On October 7, 1876.
His men built shelters near its banks,
With buffalo hides and sticks.

"I'll ride about the countryside,"
He said, "and try to find our prey.
We've come to get some buffalo hides
And we must not delay."

He rode the circuit south and west
Till the sun was sinking low.
When he topped a hill a mile from camp,
He saw a herd of buffalo.

He gazed into the open plain,
The herd was in full sight.
'Can I be dreaming,' he said to himself,
'Or is that buffalo white?'

(continued)

He galloped back to seek an aide,
To which Dan Dowd replied,
"I'll gladly help you, Mr. Mooar,
We'll get that buffalo hide."

They slipped slowly down the creek bank
Toward the bison 'neath the tree.
The white beast loomed against the sky
Like a ship upon the sea.

He aimed, he fired, the giant fell dead,
It glistened in the setting sun.
The ground shook like thunder,
When he killed the ghostly one.

That shot no longer can be heard;
The buffalo graze our plains no more.
We have, instead, a legend,
That brings history to our door.

So J. Wright Mooar left more than fame,
His gift won't fade away.
He left the legend of the White Buffalo,
When his shot rang out that day.

Charles G. Anderson
® 1967

Notes

Chapter III
1. Mooar, J. Wright (as told to James Winford Hunt), "Buffalo Days, The Chronicle Of An Old Hunter," *Holland's*, Vol. 52 No. 1, January, 1933, p. 24.

2. ibid

3. ibid

Chapter VII
4. Op cit, Vol. 52 No. 2, February, 1933, p. 44.

Chapter X
5. Op cit, Vol. 52 No. 3, March, 1933, p. 8.

Chapter XI
6. Nye, W.S. *Bad Medicine and Good,* University of Oklahoma Press, Norman, 1962, pp. 179-180.

Chapter XIII
7. Mooar, J. Wright (as told to James Winford Hunt), "Buffalo Days, The Chronicle Of An Old Hunter," *Hollands,* Vol. 52 No. 4, April, 1933, p. 22.

8. ibid, p. 22.

Chapter XV
9. ibid, p. 22.

Chapter XVI
10. Op cit, Vol. 52 No. 5, May, 1933, p. 11.

11. ibid, p. 11.

Chapter XVII
12. ibid, p. 11.

13. ibid, p. 8.

Chapter XX
14. Gilbert, Miles, compiler, *Getting A Stand,* Pioneer Press, Union City, Tennessee, 1993, pp. 1-16.

Bibliography

Bible. Mooar Family, Boston: Mussey, B.B., 1844, Pages of Mooar Family History (Scurry County Historical Society).

Brown, Dee. *Bury My Heart At Wounded Knee,* Holt, Rinehard, Winston, New York, 1970, pp. 263-271, 399-401.

Burton, Gerry. "Statue Of Famed White Buffalo Sought For Scurry County," *Abilene Reporter News,* February 14, 1967, p. 1, Sect. B.

Carpenter, Allan. *Arizona, From Its Glorious Past To The Present,* Children's Press, Chicago, 1966, pp. 44-45, 65.

Crane, R.C. "Creation Of Scurry & Fifty-Three Other Counties," *Scurry County Times,* 50th Anniversary Ed., December 30, 1937, p. 2, Sect. 2.

_____. "Gen. Robert E. Lee In Scurry County," *Scurry County Times* 50th Anniversary Ed., December 30, 1937, p. 14, Sect. 2.

_____. "Marcy Reconnaissance Thru West Texas," *Scurry County Times,* 50th Anniversary Ed., December 30, 1937, p. 6, Sect. 2.

Dary, David A., *The Buffalo Book,* Avon Books, New York, 1975, pp. 206-221.

Elliott, C., W.C. Pool, & L.W. Raley, "The Buffalo Slaughter," *Texas: Wilderness To Space Age,* The Naylor Co., San Antonio, 1962, pp. 408-412.

Fields, F.T., "The Frontier Forts," *Texas Sketchbook,* Humble Oil & Refining Co., January 15, 1962, pp. 78-83.

Gilbert, Miles. Compiler, *Getting A Stand,* Pioneer Press, Union City, Tennessee, 1993.

Hendrix, Roy. (Worked on J. Wright Mooar Ranch in the 1920s). Personal Interview with Charles G. Anderson, Snyder, Texas, January 3, 1973.

Hester, G.C., W. C. Nunn, & R. Henson. "The People Who Lived Here," & "How The Buffalo Were Slaughtered, " *Texas, The Story of the Lone Star State,* Henry Hold & Co., USA, 1948, pp. 6-9, 443-446.

Hunter, Marvin J., Sr. "J. Wright Mooar & John W. Mooar," *Old West,* Austin, Spring 1967, pp. 27, 55.

Izzard, Bob. *Adobe Walls Wars,* Tangleaire Press, Amarillo, Texas, 1993, pp. 18-35.

"J. Wright Mooar," *Snyder Daily News,* 75th Anniversary Ed., Snyder, Texas, Dec. 9, 1962, p. 10, Sect. 3.

"J. Wright Mooar," *Snyder Daily News,* Snyder, Texas, October 11, 1953, p. 1, Sect. 7.

Mayer, Frank H. & Charles B. Roth. *The Buffalo Harvest,* Pioneer Press, Union City, Tennessee, 1995, pp. 11-22, 84-89.

Newman, Jason. "Dallas Historical Society To Research Rath City Lore," *Abilene Reporter News,* Abilene, Texas, January 27, 1996, pp.1-8.

_____. "Team Scouting Bones Of Buffalo Boom Town," *Abilene Reporter News,* Abilene, Texas, February 3, 1996, p. 2A.

Nye, W.S., Bad Medicine and Good, Univ. of Oklahoma Press, Norman, 1962, pp. 179-180.

McGlaun, June, et al. "History of Scurry County," *McGlaun Room Times,* Pub. 4th Grade Students, West Elem. School, October 17, 1967, Snyder, Texas, pp. 1-5.

Mooar, J. Wright (as told to Jas. Winford Hunt). "Buffalo Days, The Chronicle of An Old Buffalo Hunter," *Holland's,* Vol. 52, Nos. 1-5, January-May, 1933.

Paddock, B.B. "J. Wright Mooar," *Texas Grand Lodge Magazine,* Vol. 30, August, 1960, Waco, pp. 275-279. (First pub. in *Biographical History of North & West Texas,* 1906).

"Pete Snyder, Founder of Settlement," *Snyder Daily News,* 75th Anniversary Ed., Snyder, Texas, December 9, 1962, p. 10, Sect. 8.

Richardson, Rupert N. *Texas, The Lone Star State,* Prentice-Hall, Inc., New York, 1943, pp. 300-308.

    _____. "The Battle of Adobe Walls, 1874," *The Battles of Texas*,
        The Texian Press, Waco, 1967, pp. 175-189.

Shelton, Hooper. *From Buffalo to Oil: A History of Scurry County, Texas*,
        Feather Printing Co., Snyder, Texas, 1973, p. 19.

Thompson, Louise. "The Trail Of A Buffalo Hunter, J. Wright Mooar,"
        English Paper, Hardin-Simmons Univ., Abilene,
        December 10, 1964.

Webb, Walter P. "Animal Life on the Great Plains," *The Great Plains*, Gun &
        Co., Boston, 1931, p. 44.

Wright, Hamilton. "Snyder In Transition," *Ft. Worth Star Telegram*,
        June 22, 1962, n/p, (Scurry County Historical Society).

* * *

THE LAST HOME OF J. WRIGHT MOOAR. Located one block from the old Snyder school, Wright moved here from his ranch on Deep Creek so that his granddaughter, Judy, would be close to the school. Mooar died in this house on 26th Street on May 1, 1940. (Photo by the author Charles G. Anderson).

INDEX

Legend: Photo..(P.) Map...(Map) Art/Illustration..(Art)

Adobe Walls...44, 46, 48
    Battle...54-65
    Site...(P. 54, 58, 59)
    Monument..64, (P. 57)
Aiken, George...80

Ainsworth, Beverly...110
Allen-Noah, Francene...113
Anchutz, D. W. (P. 45)
Anderson, Charles G. ...(P. 130)
Antelope Jack (John Thomson Jones)...44
Anthony, A.J. (Store)...(P. 22)
Aparapahos...53, 76
Arizona Territory...101
    Phoenix...101
    Prescott...101
Arkansas River...viii, 26
    Bridge (Dodge City) (P. 35)
Armitage, Harry...55

Bell, William...(P. 124)
Berry, Will...116
Best-Son-In-Law...64
Big Fifty Sharps...46, (P. 115, 118-119)
Big Tree (Ado-Etta) 68, (P.72)
Billingsley, Hack..(P. 126)
Billy the Kid...91
Black Beaver (Delaware)...75
Black Horse.(P. 65)
Blue Billy...44
Blum, John Dr. ...118
Boomers Camp...(P. 74)
Boren, Hugh (Brud) Jr. ...iii, 92, (P.130)
Boren, Wayne...(P. 113)
Born, "Dutch Henry"...55
Brazos River...78
Brown, Frank...55

Buffalo... 31, (P. 42),
    Uses by Indians...18
    Herds... (P. 28, 32)
    Hides.... (P. 47)
    Hunters' Camp...(P. 93)
    Ranges...(Map 33, 39)
    Skinning...(P. 75)
    Slaughter...(P. 19)

Buffalo Bill...23, (P. 67)
Buffalo Gap, Texas... (P. 49)
Buffalo Hunting (Currier & Ives)... (Art 21)
Byrd, Grandpa...124

Camp Reynolds...80, 91
Campbell, James...55
Canadian River...41, 44, 52, 88
Caprock, The (Texas)...13, (P.81-82)
Carlisle, "Burmuda"...55
Cator, James H. ...57
Chapman, Amos...48-49, 54
Cheyenne...53, 64
    Agency (I.T.)...68
Chief-Stone-Cav-Son...64
Chiricahua Apaches...101
Cimarron River...40, 66
Clear Fork Brazos River...iii, 78
Coble, Mr. & Mrs. W.T. ...57
Colorado City, Texas...104, (Map 111)
Colorado River...78,
Comanches...53
Comancheros...43
Cotton, Fred...(P. 126)

138

Cottonwood Creek...95
Courthouse (Scurry Co., Texas)
    1886...(P. 124)
Coyote...64
Creek, Red Deer...44
Delaware (Indians)...75
Dallas, Texas...76
Davis, E.J. ...72
Deep Creek...13, 80, 82, (P. 87, 95)
Denson, Dewey...(P. 126)
Dixon, Billy (Wm.)... 55, 56
    Dixon, Mrs. Billy...57
Dodge City, Kansas... 26, 66
    Ft. Dodge, 1870... (P. 22)
Dodge, Richard I. Col. Maj...37, 38
Double Mtn. Fork...80, 91-92, 95
Dowd, Dan...83-84, 86, 133
Dudley, Dave...44
Dugout...(P. 90)
Dull Knife, Chief...(P. 25)
"Dutch Henry" Born...55

Eastman Bus.College..19
Eddy, George...55
Emerson, Bill...116
Ennis Creek...96
Ennis, James (Jim)...91

"Frenchy"_____ ...55
Fifty Sharps Rifle...46
First Methodist Church...106
Freight Wagons...(P. 102)
Ft. Clark, Texas...62
Ft. Griffin, Tx...75-76, (P. 78), 102
Ft. Hays, Kansas...vii, (P. 16)
Ft. Phantom Hill, Tx...77, (P. 79)
Ft. Worth, Texas...76-77

Garrett, Pat...91
Gavitte...96
Geronimo...101
    & Son...(P. 94)
Goff, John...95
Goodnight Ranch...(P. 42)
Grant, Old Man...(P. 124)
Grantham, Walter...(P. 124)
Green, J.W...(P. 124)

Green, Randall H. & Sons...18

Haley, J. Evetts...92
Hamlin, Texas...80

Hanrahan, Jas. (Jim)...44, 49, 55
    Saloon... (Art 54)
Hart, Charley...96
Hays, S.D. & Judy...(P. 117)
    Judy... 114, (P. 85, 98, 115,
    119, 129, 131)
Hell Roarin' Holler, Texas...126
Hendrix, Roy... 92
Henry Rifle (Mooar's)...(P. 118)
Heritage Museum (Texas)...116
Hide Town,Texas...106
Horse-Chief...64
Howard's Well, Texas... 62
Hunt, John (Cabin)...34, 35
Hunting/Mooar's Travels (Map.39)
Hutchinson Co.,Texas...57

Indian Territory... (P. 74)
Indians, Plains... (P. 40)
Isa-tai....56, 63, (P. 65), 70

Johnson, Andrew...55
Jones, C.E."Dirty Face"...54, 55
Jones, John Thomson
    (Antelope Jack)...44

Kansas & Pacific RR...(P. 23)
Kayser, "Mule"...116
Keeler, Old Man...55
Kelton, Elmer...(P. 130)
Kiowa Creek...34
Kiowa...53
Koch, Augustus...111
Kutch, Ira...(P. 124)
Kwahadi Comanche...60

Lane & Wheeler...43
Langton, James...55, 57
Lease, Henry...55, 63
Lee & Reynolds...79, 80
Lee, Robert E. Gen....14
Leonard, Fred...44, 55

139

Llano Estacado...43
Lone Wolf (Gui-pah-go)...(P. 61), 67
Lumpkins, Thomas (Tom)...80
Mackenzie, Ranald S...117
Marcy, Randolph B...14 (P. 15), 80
Masterson, Bat
   (Wm. Bartholomew)...55
McCabe, Mike...55
McDonnell, Mamie...(P. 113)
   Grave Site...(P. 128)
McDonnell, Tommy...(P. 113, 121),
   (Grave Site...128)
McDow, Earl...92
McKinley, James...55
Medicine Lodge Treaty (1867)...36,
   40, 43, 56
Mescalero Apaches...101, (P. 94)
Myer's Store (Art 54)
Miles, Nelson Gen. (P. 67, 71), 68
Mitchell Co., Texas...110
Monroe, Jody...(P. 121)
Mooar... 79, 108, (P. 113)
   Adobe Walls...44, 49
   Birthplace, (Pownal, Vermont)...
   (P. 14)
   Brothers & Wright Co...22, 34, 42
     Campsite... (P. 80)
     Deep Creek...82
     Grave Site...(P. 127)
     Guns... (P. 115-121)
     Historical Markers...
       Town...(P. 122)
       Hwy. 84...(P. 123)
     Homes...
       Ranch...97, (P. 112-114)
       Town (26th St)...(P. 137)
     Livery Stable (P. 105)
     Travels...(Map 17, 77)
     Water Well... (P. 98)
     Whirlwind...68
     White Buf. Hide...(P. Cover, 86)
     Other: (P. 120, 121)
Mooar, Esther K. ...13, (P. 108)
Mooar, J. W. Bros. ... (P. 104)
Mooar, J. Wright & Julia...(P. 107)
Mooar, J. Wright... (P. x, 108,
   120-121, 129)
Mooar, John... (P. 20)
   Adobe Walls...44, 48
   Ft. Phantom Hill...79
   Jewelry Business (N.Y)...18
Mooar, John Allen...13, (P. 108)
                Mooar,
John W. Jr...(P. 125)
Mooar, Julia Swartz...(P. 108)
   Grave Site...(P. 127)
Mooar, Lydia Louise "Dot"..(P. 125)
Moore...96
Moore, J.P. & Sons...116
Morrison, Ralph (body)... (P. 53)
Mulberry Creek...34, 66
Mule Teams/RR...(P. 103)
Murphy, Martin...(P. 126)
Myers, Charlie...44
   Store... (Art 54)

Natchez...(P. 94)
Negro Bugler...63
Neuces River, Texas...(P. 94)
Neutral Strip (Indian Territory)...43
Newhouse, B.K....iii
Nocona, Peta...60
Nunn Brothers...103
Nunn, Jim...(P. 124)
Nunn, Tommy...110

O'Keefe's Blacksmith
   Shop.. (Art. 54)
O'Keefe, Thomas...44, 49, 55
Ogg, Billy...55
Olds, William...55, 57
   Grave Site...P. 66)
Olds, Mrs. William (Hannah)... 55,
   57, 64

Palo Duro Canyon...43, 67
Panhandle (Texas)...41, 42, 44
Parker, Quanah...vii, 49, 54,
   66, 89, 115, (P. 60, 65, 88)
Patterson, H.B (Houston)...110
Philadelphia...76, 124

Pierce, Robert, Dr...(P. 118)
Pony Express...26
Poughkeepsie, N.Y....19
Powell, R.T...110
Pownal, Vermont...13
Rath, Charles...44, 79, 80, (P. 47)
    Rath City...80, 91
    Rath's Store...(Art 54)
    Rath & Wright's
        hide yard... (P. 47)
    Rath and Wright's Store...57
Red Deer Creek...51
Reynolds, Camp...80
Richards, J.J. & J.M
    Jewelry Bus. (N.Y)....19
Robber's Roost,Texas...106
Rochelle, Illinois...16
Roosevelt, Theodore...105
Roscoe, Snyder & Pacific Railroad
    (R.S. & P. RR)...(P. 124)
Russell, John...79, 80

Satank...72
Satanta, Chief...68, (P. 72)
Scurry County...91, 105
Scurry, William R. Gen....105
Serpent-Scales...64
Shadler Brothers...57
    Isaac "Ike"...55, 56
    Jacob "Shorty"...55, 56
Sharps Rifles...(P. 115-117)
Shepherd, (Will)...55
Sing, Charlie...80
Sisk, Phillip...46
Si-Ta-Do...64
Slue-Foot...64
Smith, "Limpy Jim"...80
Smith, Oz...(P. 124)
Smith, Sam...55
Smoke House...99
Snyder, William Henry,
    "Pete"... (P.24), 99, 110
    Pete & Nellie (P. 96)
    Grave Sites...(P. 128)
    Ranch...(P. 126)
Snyder, Texas, (1883)...(Map. 110)

(1904)...(P. 109)
    Cemetery...(P. 106)
    Courthouse (1911)...(P. 109)
    Masonic Lodge...106
Soft-Foot...64
Solomon, H.R...110
Sonoran Desert...102
Southern Pacific RR..(P. 94), 101
Spotted-Feather...64
Springfield Army Rifle...43
Stone-Teeth...64
Swartz, Julia Mrs. ...105
Sweetwater Creek...91

Taylor, Arlie...(P. 126)
Taylor, Robert...(P. 131)
Texas Centennial Parade,
    (Snyder, Texas)...(P. 121)
Texas & Pacific Railroad Co. ...103
Texas Legislature...105
Thrane, O.P. (P. 121)
Tipis... (P. 38)
Tomahakara, Monroe (Chief)
    (P. 129), (P. 131), 115
Towle, H.G. Dr. ..118, (P. 113, 121)
Townsend, 'Booger Red'...(P. 113)
Trevor, Edward...55
Turkey Track Ranch...57, 66
Tyler, Billy...55, 56

Vermont...76, 77
Victorio...101

Wagon w/hides...(P. 37)
Wagons w/hunters...(P. 49)
Wallace, Tommy...44
Warren Wagontrain...68
Watson, Hiram...55
Weathers, Ben...116
Webb, John...41
Welch, Mike...55
West Texas hillside... (P.100)
Wheeler...44
Whirlwind, Chief...vii, 67-72,
    (P. 69), 73
White Buffalo ...81-87
    Hide...(P. Cover, 86)

       Poem...132
       Site... (P.83, 85)
       Statues
           1967...(P.131)
           1994...(P. i, 114, 131)
White Horse (Kiowa
       Sub-Chief)... (P. 62)
Wichita Indian Agency...75
Wild Horse...64, 67, (P. 65)
Wilmeth, A.C. ...(P. 121)
Wilson, Lem...46, 52
Wolf-Tongue...64
Womack, B.F. Sr. & Mrs. ...(P. 113)
Wood, A.R. (P. 105)
Wood, Az...(P. 124)
Wright, Charles...22, 42
Wright, Robert M. ...79, 80
       Store...(P. 22)
Wylks, Frank...(P. 124)

Zimmerman, F.C. ...116_